Grow the Core

Grow the Core

How to Focus on Your Core Business for Brand Success

David Taylor

A John Wiley & Sons, Ltd., Publication

Registered office

John Wiley & Sons Ltd, The Atrium, Southern Gate, Chichester, West Sussex, PO19 8SQ, United Kingdom

For details of our global editorial offices, for customer services and for information about how to apply for permission to reuse the copyright material in this book please see our website at www.wiley.com.

Wiley publishes in a variety of print and electronic formats and by print-on-demand. Some material included with standard print versions of this book may not be included in e-books or in print-on-demand. If this book refers to media such as a CD or DVD that is not included in the version you purchased, you may download this material at http://booksupport.wiley.com. For more information about Wiley products, visit www.wiley.com.

Designations used by companies to distinguish their products are often claimed as trademarks. All brand names and product names used in this book are trade names, service marks, trademarks or registered trademarks of their respective owners. The publisher is not associated with any product or vendor mentioned in this book.

Library of Congress Cataloging-in-Publication Data

Taylor, David, 1964-
    Grow the core : how to focus your core business for brand success / David
    Taylor.
        pages cm
    Includes bibliographical references and index.
    ISBN 978-1-118-48471-5 (hbk)
1. Brand name products–Management. 2. Product management. 3. Strategic planning.
4. Branding (Marketing) I. Title.
    HD69.B7T396 2013
    658.8′27–dc23

                                                            2012042402

A catalogue record for this book is available from the British Library.

ISBN 978-1-118-48471-5 (hbk) ISBN 978-1-118-48468-5 (ebk)
ISBN 978-1-118-48469-2 (ebk) ISBN 978-1-118-48470-8 (ebk)

Set in 12/15pt Garamond by Laserwords Private Limited, Chennai, India
Printed in Great Britain by TJ International Ltd, Padstow, Cornwall, UK

*To Mum and Dad, for your support,
encouragement and inspiration.*

Contents

Thanks

First and foremost, thanks to the brand leaders with whom I have been lucky enough to work on Growing the Core. A special mention to the Marketing Directors who have invited me to coach them and their teams on their portfolios of brands: Ian Penhale at SAB Miller, Phil Chapman at Kerry Foods, Carol Welch at Jordans Ryvita, Maria Grigorova at Mars, Steve Brass and Bill Noble at WD-40.

Thanks to the Wiley team for helping create the *brandgym* series of books that allow us to share our branding tips, tools and tricks with a global audience. In particular, thanks to Claire Plimmer for securing the initial go-ahead to publish *Grow the Core* and to Iain Campbell for his excellent editing input and advice.

Thanks to my old boss and marketing mentor Mark Sherrington for publishing an earlier, shorter version of *Grow the Core* in eBook form on his digital publishing platform, Shoulders of Giants.

Thanks to Professor Byron Sharp for his breakthrough book *How Brands Grow*, which has been a source of inspiration, especially opening my eyes to the importance of distinctiveness and penetration.

A special thanks to my brilliant business partner and buddy David Nichols, who, yet again, gave invaluable feedback to focus and sharpen the key ideas.

Thanks to the other *brandgym* partners, Anne Charbonneau in Amsterdam, Diego Kerner and Silvina Moronta in Buenos Aries and Prasad Narasimhan in Bangalore for their input and ideas.

Finally, thanks to the people who read the first six books in the *brandgym* series and took the time to write and tell me that you liked them and found them useful. Your positive feedback kept me going when the going got tough writing this book.

Introduction

A strong core is essential for success. This is true for brands as much as it is for physical fitness. An increasing number of people in your local gym are trying to improve their 'core strength' by working out the muscles deep in the abs and back that help keep the body stable and balanced.

In the same way, a strong core is also important for keeping a business healthy and in shape. Indeed, most successful businesses are built on a solid foundation of a core business where they have a leading position. Timberland might sell a range of clothing and accessories, but the original Timberland boot is still crucial from both a business and brand image standpoint. The same goes for Dove and its little white cleansing bar and Hellmann's with its original mayonnaise. Growing the core has many advantages. By selling more of the stuff you already do well, you grow without adding complexity. Instead, you make what is strong even stronger, both in terms of brand equity and economies of scale.

However, despite the advantages of growing the core, companies that successfully do this are in the minority. Research shows that many companies neglect their core business and, in doing so, miss out on opportunities for profitable growth (1). Instead, they over-rely on stretching away from their core with new products or services. Like the favourite elder child, brand stretch gets all the love and attention. Now, brand stretch can drive growth, as shown in my earlier book, *Brand Stretch: Why 1 in 2 extensions fail and how to beat the odds*. However, companies under-estimate just how hard it is to stretch into a new category and take on an established brand leader in *its* core market. This is why the brand stretch graveyard is over-flowing with failed launches, such as Levi's suits,

Bic perfumes and Cosmopolitan yoghurts. Worse still are the new launches that survive but end up being 'brand dwarves'; small products or services that add little in extra sales, but increase complexity for retail partners, consumers and the company itself.

All of this risks dilution of core brand equity as the brand has to communicate multiple benefits. It also creates fragmentation of the brand's sales, with these being spread over a larger number of smaller products, often leading to a dilution of profitability. It can also provoke a dangerous decline in the core business, owing to resources being diverted to support the 'new toys'. Marketing budget is taken away from the core, but just as important is the tendency for the best talent in the team and senior management to be distracted from the core business.

In contrast, growing your core makes what is strong even stronger, both in terms of your brand and business, and it does this without adding any complexity. However, if growing the core is so powerful, why is it underutilised? Well, one reason is that it can just seem less sexy than new product development. Innovation with a capital 'I' is what hits the headlines, with companies feeling compelled to create new products and services that take their brands in new directions. The tendency in the past has been for new launches to attract a greater share of the rewards and faster career advancement for those involved.

Another reason growing the core is often forgotten about is because it's actually hard, requiring just as much, if not more, creativity than designing and launching new products. Most marketing people have been trained on how to develop, test and launch a new product. If you need some help, there are 45 000 books about innovation on Amazon, plus countless conferences and seminars to attend. In contrast, there is little or no practical advice about selling more of the stuff you already make. This is clear from the blank looks I get when I ask a typical team to create 10 ways to grow their core, without new products or services. That's where this book comes in.

The first part of this book answers the question '**Why Grow the Core?**'. In the first chapter I address the important task of **Defining the core**, which companies often find is not straightforward. You will see how to do this based on identifying your brand's 'source of authority', often the product that made you famous in the first place, and your 'source of profit'. **Stretching the brand, forgetting the core** explores the risks of over-relying on brand stretch for growth, both in terms of the high failure rate and the risk of resources being diverted from your core to fund brand stretching. Part I ends with **The case for the core**, exploring the advantages of this route to growth, including how it reinforces what made you famous and creates economies of scale.

In Part II, I introduce the **Grow the Core Principles**. First, you will be introduced to the three **growth drivers** that can help you grow your core business. The first driver is using distinctive marketing to create 'fresh consistency'. Consistency comes from creating and amplifying distinctive brand properties that work as a unifying force. Freshness comes from waves of marketing activity that deliver 'new news', including communication, product and activation. The second driver is increasing distribution to make the core available in more places, using both existing and new channels. Importantly, these first two types of core growth both help you sell more stuff, 'SMS' for short. They require no additional products or services, but rather increase revenue from what you already have. The third and final growth driver is core extension, both through new packaging formats and products. I complete Part II by exploring the difference between **renovation** and **re-invention**. This will help you assess the right balance between freshness and consistency for your core, based on the health of your brand and the category in which it operates. At one extreme, there is the need to renovate a healthy brand; at the other end is the most challenging case of all, re-inventing the core to respond to dramatic and potentially deadly changes to the market as a whole.

In Part III, I explore in detail the six **Grow the Core Workouts**. The first four workouts focus on distinctive marketing using your **product**, **identity**, **communication** and **activation**. Next is how to use **distribution** in both **current** and **new channels**. I then explore how to extend the core via **added value products** and **formats**.

In Part IV, I share **A workplan to Grow the Core**. This practical guide will help you implement the principles and workouts in your business. You will discover how to get deep **Insight** about your brand, business and consumer and use this as fuel for generating **Ideas** to grow the core. The **Exploration** stage reveals the best ways of bringing these ideas to life and exploring them with consumers. Finally, in the **Action** stage you will discover a novel approach to priority setting that borrows from the world of venture capital.

As with the previous six books in the *brandgym* series, *Grow the Core* is meant to be a practical business-building toolkit. It should live on your desk, rather than sitting on a shelf or by your bedside table. Keep it close by. The emphasis is on tips, tools and tricks that have been road-tested on real-life projects with my consultancy, *the brandgym*. Every key point is illustrated with at least one brand example to bring it to life. Visit *brandgymblog.com* to find more detail on the case studies, including examples of TV advertising, and packaging and digital activation.

WHY GROW THE CORE?

PART I

Defining the core

 Headlines

At the heart of most strong brands is a strong core product or service. This strong core is a profitable source of growth in its own right and also the foundation on which future initiatives can be built, so it plays a crucial role. An important first step is to define what the core is, by identifying your brand's source of both profit and authority.

What *is* the core?

Most successful brands started out by selling one thing. Dove was once a single, simple cleansing bar. Apple sold computers. Virgin was a record company. There are some brands that have stuck to a mono-product proposition, making the core easy to identify. The Coca-Cola brand still sells only cola, for example, with the company using other brands for different products: innocent for smoothies, Powerade for sports drinks, Sprite for lemonade and so on.

However, other brands now sell lots of things. Back to the earlier examples, Dove sells a range of beauty-care products, including shampoos, deodorants and shower gels. Apple sells iPods, iPhones and iPads and is a leading retailer. And Virgin is perhaps the world's most stretched brand. This proliferation of brand extensions makes it increasingly difficult to define the core. In my client work I often come across teams who find 'What is the core?' a much more challenging question than you would expect. Of course, if you don't know what the core is, you haven't got a hope in hell of growing it!

There are two key questions you can use to define the core of your brand: what is your number one source of profit and what is your source of authority?

Follow the money

At the most fundamental level, the core product or service is the big, often the biggest, bit of business. So when you're trying to identify the core, a good place to start is to use *the brandgym's* favourite motto and 'follow the money'. For example, Hellmann's has stretched into many new areas such as dips and sauces but the original mayonnaise still makes up most of the sales. Although the Dove brand has stretched into many new categories, the soap bar business still represents an important part of the brand's sales. In addition, core products are often more profitable. The core business is one that the company masters thanks to many years of experience and the size of the business means that there are often important economies of scale. Furthermore, as the brand is well known and trusted in its core area, it may need less marketing support relative to sales, compared to stretching into new markets where the brand is less well known.

Producing a portfolio map like the one in Figure 1.1 helps you follow the money and identify your core business. This simple visualisation dramatises just how important the core is. Even more interesting is when the marketing spend allocation is added, as this is often focused on the newer, smaller products while the core is neglected. Have you got this sort of analysis for your brand? If not, doing this exercise is a good start to helping you define your core business.

What made you famous?

The core product is also a source of authority. The brand's key attributes, benefits and associations are tied up in it. Often,

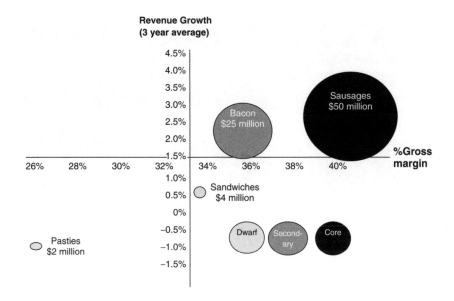

Figure 1.1: 'Following the money' for a food company.
(Source: author's own).

this is the original product that the brand started out with. For example, Johnson & Johnson now has a broad range of products, yet most US consumers still think of the baby shampoo when asked about the brand. Timberland now sells a whole range of clothing and accessories, but the boot is still emblematic of the brand, the 'hero product' of the range (Figure 1.2) and the foundation for the whole business. You can see this in the company's philosophy (1):

> Historically, Timberland's evolution has been framed by the theme of 'Boot, Brand, Belief'. 'Boot' is represented by founder Nathan Swartz, who created the company's iconic waterproof leather boot. His son Sidney Swartz built the Timberland 'Brand', expanding the company internationally and adding product lines such as apparel, women's and children's footwear, and accessories such as backpacks and watches.

Smirnoff Ice might be a faster growing part of the Smirnoff brand, but the company still invests heavily in the core vodka. As with any innovation and parent brand,

Figure 1.2: Example of a 'hero' core product. Reproduced by permission of Timberland LLC.

Smirnoff Red vodka brings stature and credibility to its extension. This is an important difference versus new pre-mixed drink brands such as Reef that have no spirit heritage. The Dove brand team went as far as implementing controls to ensure that new extensions were introduced only after two 'traffic lights' had gone green, based on brand equity tracking studies:

i) a strong soap bar business had been built;
ii) the brand had satisfactory scores on attribute ratings for mildness and moisturisation.

What is your brand's source of authority, what advantages does it bring you and what are you doing to protect it?

Your core

Hopefully by now, having reviewed your brand and business, including the source of authority and source of profit, you will have identified your core. Be careful not to get too bogged down in intellectual debates about this issue though. I have seen some teams end up in an almost philosophical debate about what the core really is. Put most simply, growing the core is about a focus on selling more of the stuff you already sell, as an alternative to growing by launching new products and services. We call this 'SMS' for short (Sell More Stuff).

Anchoring the core

In many cases, within the core product range there is an 'anchor' version: the simplest, purest version of the brand. These anchor versions are often labelled 'Classic' or 'Original'. For Special K, Kellogg's breakfast cereal, the plain flavour is the anchor version. The wide range of flavour extensions, such as Red Berries, Peach & Apricot and Strawberry & Chocolate can be positioned against this original version. They can focus on emphasising specific attributes and benefits, rather than communicating the whole product concept. So, as a consumer, we would say 'Oh, it's Special K with a bit of added flavour'.

Budweiser the brand has Budweiser the product as its anchor. It's not called Bud Original or Bud Classic. Just Bud. This original version has been around since 1879 and the pack identity has stayed consistent over this time. It stars in ongoing product-quality communication, selling the benefits of fresh beer. Satellite extensions, or 'planets', like Bud Light can then orbit around this 'sun' and draw on its authentic imagery.

The anchor version often declines as new variants are launched, but the 'original' or 'classic' versions remain an important source of credibility on which the extensions can rely (Table 1.1). Anchor versions are often the 'star product' when a brand wants to communicate a brand message, rather than a product-specific one. The traditional red and white of Classic Coke and iconic glass 'contour' bottle are featured in the brand's advertising and sponsorship of major sporting events, such as the soccer World Cup. This is Coke's strategy despite the fact that, in many markets, Diet

Core
extension =
Cherry Coke

Anchor =
Classic
Coke

Core
extension =
Diet Coke

Figure 1.3: Anchor product and core extensions for Coke.

Table 1.1: Anchor versions

Masterbrand	Core Product	Anchor Version	Other Versions
Bacardi	Rum	Carta Blanca	Limon, Bacardi 8 (aged)
Special K	Cereal	Plain	Strawberry & Chocolate, Red Berries
Marlboro	Cigarettes	Red top	Light, Medium, Ultra Light
Smirnoff	Vodka	Red	Black
Dove	Soap bar	Original blue	Sensitive, Refreshing green

Coke/Coke Light is actually bigger in sales than Classic Coke (Figure 1.3).

Some brands don't have a single anchor version. This is the case when brands are built on the idea of offering variety and choice. An example is the Clairol Herbal Essences shampoo range, which has different versions for different hair types. In this case, there isn't a clearly identified anchor version.

Key takeouts

1. Most strong brands have at their heart a strong core product.
2. The core can be defined based on the source of profit and the source of authority.
3. The anchor version is the simplest, purest incarnation of the core product, against which other core extensions can be positioned.

 Checklist 1. Defining the core

	Yes	No
• Have you defined your core, based on source of authority and source of profit?	☐	☐
• Are the team and senior management aligned such that this core will be the focus of your efforts to 'SMS' (sell more stuff)?	☐	☐
• Within this core range, are you clear about the anchor version (sun) against which you can position future extensions (planets)?	☐	☐

 Handover

You have now seen how to define the core of your brand based on the source of authority and source of profit and learnt about the key role played by the anchor version. In the next chapter you will discover the risks of forgetting the core and over-relying on brand stretching for growth.

Stretching the brand, forgetting the core

CHAPTER 2

 Headlines

Many companies over-rely on stretching into new markets to grow and, in doing so, forget about the core. In reality, brand stretching is much harder to do well than most teams realise. In many ways they forget what made their core business successful, expecting brand values alone to be enough to win in the new market. Furthermore, the new launches that do survive are often small 'dwarf' extensions. These pose a serious risk for the core business, diverting both management talent and financial investment.

Getting it right ... brand stretch can work – Apple

Brand stretch is a hot topic for marketing teams. And there is no doubting that when you get it right, brand stretch can drive brand and business growth. Apple's stretch beyond the core Mac computer business with the iPod, iPhone and iPad has transformed the business. Revenues in the quarter to December 2011 of $45 billion were a staggering five times the level of those in the same quarter only four years earlier, and the iPad and iPhone now account for over 70% of the company's revenues (1). Importantly, this success has come from leveraging the key strengths of the core to enter or create

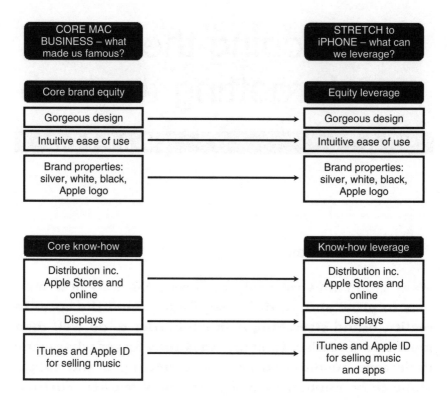

Figure 2.1: Leveraging the core when stretching.

new markets, both in terms of brand equity and know-how (Figure 2.1). Apple also had the incredible fortune to have been blessed with not one, but two creative geniuses in CEO Steve Jobs and design supremo Jonathan Ive.

Brand stretching can also work in consumer goods, not just technology markets. For example, Special K stretched from breakfast cereals into cereal snack bars (Figure 2.2) in 2001 and this business has grown to be worth almost £30 million in the UK alone. Again, Special K remembered what made the core business famous – shape management and cereals – and leveraged this in the new market of cereal bars. The company was also able to build on experience gained in cereal bars through the earlier launch of NutriGrain and Rice Krispies Squares. This meant Special K benefited from

Figure 2.2: Special K stretching from the core.

economies of scale, a distribution model that got to smaller 'impulse' outlets and in-store dominance.

Getting it wrong … brand ego tripping – Virgin

However, Apple and Special K are rare examples of successfully stretching beyond the core. The harsh reality is that your new product is more likely to end up in the over-crowded brand stretch graveyard than it is to be the next iPad or iPhone (Figure 2.3). Less than 50% of brand-stretching attempts survive after three years. In other words, you'd be better off betting your brand-stretch budget at the roulette table on black. Or red. At least then you would have a one in two chance of winning.

The reasons for this poor performance and how to increase chances of success were explored in detail in my earlier book, *Brand Stretch*. We will take a look at a brief summary of the key problem with most brand-stretching efforts: '*brand ego tripping*'. Here, you forget what made your core successful and fail to leverage your core brand equities and know-how in the new market you're stretching into. You mistakenly think that emotional brand values alone will be enough to add value in the new market. Perhaps the biggest and best example of brand ego tripping is Virgin. It is often portrayed as *the* example of how to grow by stretching beyond your core. But dig a little deeper and you find another side to the story.

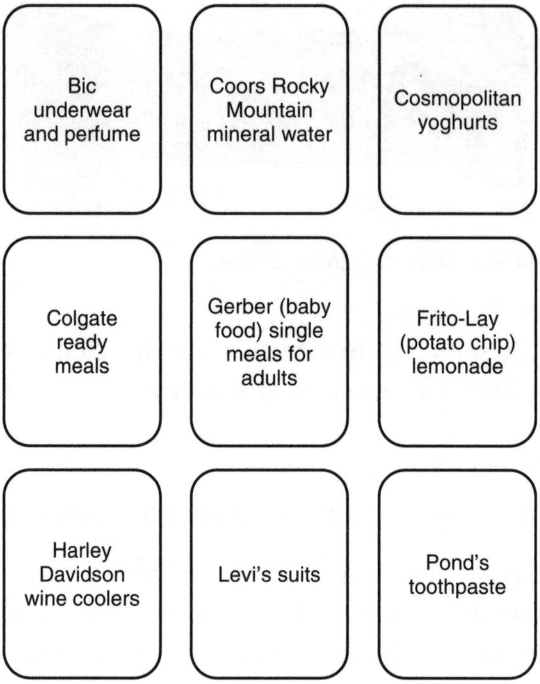

Bic underwear and perfume	Coors Rocky Mountain mineral water	Cosmopolitan yoghurts
Colgate ready meals	Gerber (baby food) single meals for adults	Frito-Lay (potato chip) lemonade
Harley Davidson wine coolers	Levi's suits	Pond's toothpaste

Figure 2.3: The extension graveyard.

Taken as a whole, Virgin is a big business, with a total group turnover of over $5 billion. However, the brand is a disparate and sprawling mass of more than 25 companies selling everything from lingerie to life insurance. Some of these businesses are shining stars, but there are just as many howling dogs. To understand the reasons for this we need to look at what made Virgin famous in the first place, and then see how they often forgot this when extending.

For the first 20 years, Virgin focused on building two businesses that created the core of the brand. One half of this core is the brand's birthplace of music, with the first Virgin record store being opened on Oxford Street in 1971. The company subsequently created its own record label in 1973. These rock 'n' roll roots give the brand its youthful, rebellious and fun-loving personality.

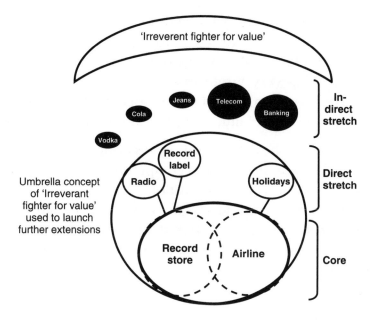

Figure 2.4: Virgin's stretch from a two-part core.

The second part of the core is the Virgin Atlantic airline that, alone, accounts for about 40% of the brand's turnover. The launch of Virgin Atlantic in 1984 gave an important second set of values: offering superior value by fighting the big boys like BA and the travel business expanded by launching Virgin Holidays in 1985.

By the end of the 1980s, Virgin's core was no longer in music or travel, but somehow a mix of the two. It had become what I call an 'irreverent, fun-loving, fighter for value'. From the 1990s, Virgin has stretched beyond this core and launched many extensions (Figure 2.4). The most recent of these extensions is the launch of a UK high-street bank, Virgin Money, through the purchase of Northern Rock's banking assets from the UK government.

This explosion of extensions is held up as *the* example of brand stretch by many branding experts. Virgin is described as a 'philosophy' or 'lifestyle' brand that can stretch into pretty much any market by leveraging its emotional 'sizzle'.

The brand is unbound by banalities such as functional product performance, or 'sausage'. However, as Professor Mark Ritson of London Business School commented in *Marketing* magazine, 'For every Virgin Atlantic or Virgin Music Group, there have been numerous failures such as Virgin Cola'. The reasons for the high failure rate fall into two main areas:

1. Size of prize: how big the business opportunity is based on market size, growth and competitive intensity, plus the strength of the value proposition.
2. Ability to win: can the business model generate sustainable, profitable growth based on cost position, route-to-market, in-store leadership and sustained marketing support?

Size of prize

Many of the Virgin brand-stretching efforts flopped as they failed to leverage the core brand equities and know-how to add value in the new market. Instead, Virgin Cola, Virgin Vodka and Virgin Jeans relied on the brand's emotional lifestyle values. However, slapping the Virgin logo on unremarkable products was not enough to take on the established Leader Brands, Coca-Cola, Smirnoff and Levi's, in *their* respective core markets.

Virgin's brand stretching worked better when it leveraged its core brand equity and know-how in new markets with a strong, functional product 'sausage' (Figure 2.5) and not just emotional 'sizzle'. This has been much easier in service businesses, where Virgin has played Robin Hood, taking on the over-charging and under-delivering bullyboys. For example, Virgin Atlantic's success is not down to people flying on it because they buy into a philosophy, but because it's a bloody good product at a competitive price. A multitude of features such as on-board massages, free ice creams and high-tech

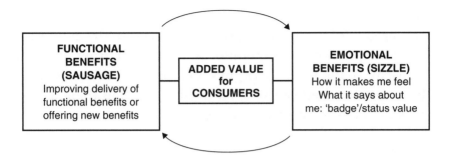

Figure 2.5: Adding value for the consumer.

video games deliver relevant differentiation. Beyond airlines, Virgin has made good inroads into the mobile phone market in the UK, USA and India. Its irreverent personality helps, but this is backed up with real service differentiation such as low-frill phones, web-based ways of buying air-time and no long-term contracts. It will be interesting to see how success-ful Virgin is in trying to deliver better banking, a market the brand is stretching into in 2012.

Ability to win

The second issue with the many failed Virgin businesses is to do with the executional and business issues that come when stretching beyond the core, such as cost position, route-to-market and marketing support. In the case of Virgin Cola, the brand was trying to take on the might of Coca-Cola and Pepsi and it lacked the resources to do this effectively. It under-spent in terms of advertising and was also out-muscled in terms of all-important in-store presence.

A further problem with the Virgin business model is that for many brand extensions the brand is simply licensed to a third party. This means that no matter how good the concept is on paper, the company has limited ability to influence the go-to-market execution and is not building any executional know-how over time. An example of how this back-fired badly was the mis-selling scandal at Virgin Energy. The door-to-door sales people of venture partner London Electricity hadn't read Virgin's customer service charter. They were accused of using hard-selling to flog their wares, and watchdog Energywatch received many complaints.

Focus your brand stretching

At this point it's important to say that the key message of this chapter is not to avoid brand stretching altogether. Rather, the idea is to do fewer, bigger and better brand extensions, where there is a decent size of prize and ability to win. A visual summary and detailed checklist to help you assess the size of prize and ability to win are shown in Figure 2.6 and Figure 2.7, illustrated using the Special K cereal bar example from earlier.

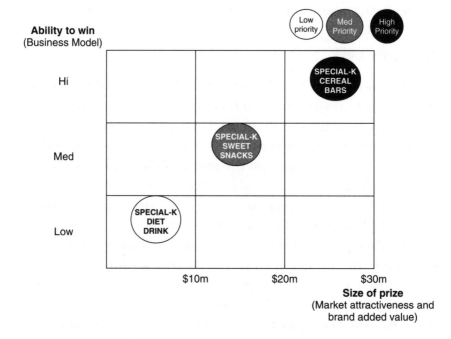

Figure 2.6: Ability to win and size of prize – summary.

Business model	Score/10	Rationale
Cost position: do we have economies of scale and manufacturing capabilities that allow a competitive cost position?	8	Economies of scale from bar factory
Route-to-market: do we have the expertise to get the product to market?	8	Expertise in supermarkets and convenience stores
In-store leadership: is the new product in part of the store where we have a strong position and influence?	9	Category captain in cereal bars
Marketing support levels: can we afford the right level of support over the long term?	8	Long term commitment to investment
SUB-TOTAL/40	33	

Ability to Win

Market attractiveness	Score/10	Rationale
Market size	7	£50million
Market growth rate	9	10% a year
Intensity of competition	9	Kellogg's dominates
SUB-TOTAL/30	25	

Brand added value	Score/10	Rationale
Concept performance: do we bring a new and relevant benefit to the market?	8	Shape mgt is new and relevant; Special K strong equity
Product/pack performance: does the product and packaging deliver against the concept?	9	Good taste in blind test, 90 calories per bar
Price/value: can we market the product at an attractive price relative to the existing offers on the market?	8	Lower grams per bar gets to attractive price point
SUB-TOTAL/30	25	

Size of Prize

Figure 2.7: Size of prize and ability to win – detail for Special K cereal bars.

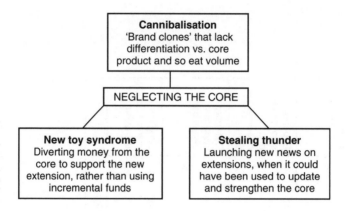

Figure 2.8: Risks for the core.

Snow White and the 17 dwarves

Failed extensions are bad for business, but the bigger threats for the core business are the small brand extensions that manage to survive. If the big, beautiful core business is 'Snow White', then these tiny, new products are like the 'seven dwarves'; only in most cases there are more like 17 of them. Whilst these dwarf products may be nice, novel and cute, they can seriously harm your core business in three main ways: stealing thunder, cannibalisation and new toy syndrome (Figure 2.8).

Stealing thunder

Brand extensions are often used to launch exciting, new innovations that would have been better off used to revitalise the core range. The basic rule when considering what to do with such product news is to ask if there is a 'trade-off' involved in the change.

When more means more

Upgrading the core product is a better route when the product change improves performance with no trade-off. This is how mainstream car makers like Ford responded to the increased demand for safety features such as ABS brakes and airbags pioneered by Volvo. Rather than creating their own safer car extensions, they integrated these features into existing models. These were first offered as optional extras, creating incremental revenue. Eventually, these features became expected in a car and were offered as standard.

When more means less

Extension in the best route when modifying the product adds some benefits, but risks undermining others. When Head & Shoulders wanted to respond to the trend for more regular hair washing, a frequent-use version was developed. It had a lower amount of active ingredient and a milder cleansing system. If this had been used to replace the original version, existing users may have been disappointed with the lower efficacy and left the brand. The new product was launched as a range extension and succeeded in building sales by about 10%, attracting new users into the brand.

Cannibalisation

As the name suggests, this is the risk of an extension eating up other family members. The biggest risk occurs with range extensions that are 'brand clones', which lack differentiation versus the existing products. Crest spent decades launching new toothpaste twists such as tartar control, gum protection and whitening. In the USA, market share halved from 50% with one product, to 25% with 50 products (2). Each introduction competed for the same usage occasion and introduced novelty value, but not enough added value to create incremental growth. What most people wanted was an 'all-in-one' version, successfully launched by Colgate as 'Colgate Total'.

Eating profits

Eating volume is bad enough. However, the story gets even worse when extensions cost more owing to extra goodies, yet fail to be priced up, resulting in a lower profit margin. So, not only does the new eat the old, but the profitability of the total business goes south. This problem often happens because the changes made cost the company more, without adding relevant benefits for the consumer. If you are really adding value, then you should be able to price up.

Launch and run

The problem of cannibalisation is made more likely by the 'revolving door' syndrome on many brand teams where new people come on-board every couple of years. The tendency is to 'launch and run': do an extension that boosts sales in the short term then move on before the cracks in the core product start to show up. The type of sales chart in Figure 2.9 is all too common. Note that much of the initial volume lift is 'pipeline' to fill up the shelves of key customers. The going level is often not as high, especially if re-purchase is poor. The new brand manager inherits the problem and often makes the same mistake: another extension that further weakens the core. And so on. You end up with the same or fewer sales, but spread over more products.

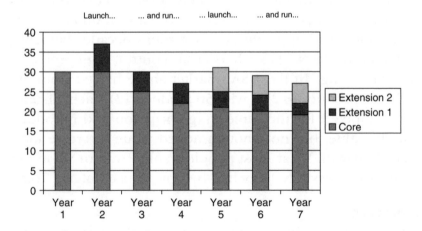

Figure 2.9: Launch and run fragments the core.

Some cannibalisation of the core will happen with most extensions, but the level can be minimised and need not be life threatening. Launching extensions that add real value is one way of doing this, as discussed earlier. However, perhaps the biggest mistake to avoid is eating into the human and financial resources of the core product.

New toy syndrome

There is always a temptation to spend time, money and energy on the sexy new extension rather than on the core business. Funds for a new extension are sometimes taken from the core range's budget, leaving it exposed to competition. In many cases, the return on investment from spending on the new extension is less than if the money had been retained on the bigger core product. As Bern Vogel, Professor of Leadership at Henley Business School, comments (3):

> In a good market you decide to buy this company or this technology – you enter a new market. It is good fun but you are doing so many activities at a time that your leadership capability is over-burdened. You lose focus and it is no longer clear what your key strengths are. Companies lose focus and do not concentrate on what they are doing well.

Companies may even cut quality on the core products over time to reduce costs and fund brand stretching. This neglect of product quality leaves the core business vulnerable to attack, as happened with the Lifebuoy soap brand in India. For decades, Lifebuoy's single, ruby-red bar delivered healthy sales growth based on delivering superior hygiene and health. However, during the 1980s and the 1990s, quality was cut until it compared poorly to competition and much of the marketing money was used to launch two new variants (Lifebuoy Plus and Lifebuoy Gold), that were less focused on the core hygiene benefit. Lifebuoy market share declined from 20% in 1996 to c. 12% several years later.

Figure 2.10: Lifebuoy: re-investing in product quality.

Fortunately, the core was re-launched in 2002, with a much richer formulation and upgraded packaging (Figure 2.10), and the Plus and Gold variants were withdrawn. Brand share climbed back up to 18.4%, making it the undisputed leader again.

Neglecting the core – Bausch & Lomb

As we have seen, brand stretching is the main way that many companies try to grow their business. When building these plans to stretch into new markets, they are often overly optimistic about the predicted sales for the core business. Many business plans feature a nice, straight line for sales of the core. However, as we saw in the last section, this obsession with brand stretch often leads to a lack of investment in the core, in terms of money, talent and product news. A more likely scenario is a slow, steady but sure decline of the core (Figure 2.11). As sales decline, budgets and investment are cut, leading to further decline.

A good example of what happens when you neglect the core is the case of Bausch & Lomb (4). In the 1980s the company built its share of new contact lens fittings to 40% by launching soft contact lenses, a market share several

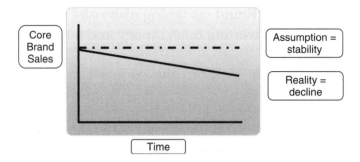

Figure 2.11: The risk of forgetting the core business.

times bigger than the nearest competitor. These lenses were healthier for users and easier to fit for eye specialists. However, the company began to divert attention away from the core, using the cash generated by this business to fund forays into new areas such as electric toothbrushes, skin ointments and hearing aids. The lack of attention and investment led to a flattening out of the core contact lens business. The share price, which had shot up from \$3 in 1973 to \$56 in 1991, dropped to less than \$33 in 2003. To make matters worse, Johnson & Johnson launched its own market-changing innovation: disposable contact lenses. Bausch & Lomb's market share declined to 16%, with the once-leader now lagging in third place behind Johnson & Johnson and Ciba Vision.

The harsh reality, as shown by this story, is that every core business is going to lose some consumers every year to competitors and just to re-fill this 'leaky bucket' a core brand needs plenty of marketing support and resources.

 Key takeouts

1. Brand stretch can help grow your brand and business, but be realistic about the chances of success: less than half of brand extensions are successful.

2. Over-relying on brand stretching also risks neglecting the core business, diverting time, money and innovation away from it.
3. Without the right support, the core will not stay stable, but rather decline.

 ## Checklist 2. Neglecting the core

	Yes	No
• Overall, do you have a commercially focused approach to brand stretching?	☐	☐
• Have you rigorously reviewed your current and planned extensions based on size of prize and ability to win?	☐	☐
• Have you maintained the level of support your core business is getting in terms of talent, budgets and innovation?	☐	☐

 ## Handover

You have now seen the risks of over-relying on brand stretching. First, the chances of success are low and your new product has more chance of ending up in the extension graveyard than being the next iPhone. In addition, you have seen how brand stretching can cause you to forget about your core business, diverting time, budgets and innovation away from it. In the next chapter I will make the case for the core by exploring the many advantages it has.

The case for the core

 Headlines

Brand stretch is not the only route to take to growth. Growing the core has many advantages over brand stretching, creating less complexity and reinforcing what made the brand famous in the first place. The case for core growth is compelling, with evidence that the majority of high-performing companies have a strong core business. Growing the core presents its own challenges, especially the need for creativity, given the lack of help and support on how to do it.

Two ways to make a million – Heinz soup

In 2007, Heinz soup stretched out of its strong core of canned soup and moved into chilled soup, with a proposition called 'Farmers' Market'. The size of prize seemed attractive; the chilled soup market was big and growing and had positive values relating to freshness and modernity. In contrast, the canned soup market was seen as being old-fashioned and lacking in food values. The concept, product and packaging for the chilled soups were pretty good and probably did well in consumer testing. There was little doubt that the Heinz brand could, in theory, stretch from canned to chilled soup. But 'can the brand stretch?' is the wrong question to ask. The right question is 'can we make any money in the new market?' and it's here that Heinz hit problems.

In terms of ability to win, Heinz was up against a dominant Leader Brand, Covent Garden, which had built a 40% share over 20 years, and premium own-label products. There were some serious issues with the business model that were perhaps overlooked or under-estimated:

1. No economies of scale in chilled soup: Heinz does canned soup really well and makes lots of it, but it had no competence in the UK in making chilled soup and small volumes. This would have put it at a cost disadvantage versus the competition.
2. Lower price: Heinz had to offer a 25% lower price vs. Covent Garden, which equalled less gross profit for marketing.
3. Trade margin: Heinz probably had to offer a better margin than Covent Garden to get listed, and this means even less profit.
4. New part of store: Heinz was entering a space where it had no presence and Covent Garden had a wall of chilled soup. What I call 'putting up a tent in front of a skyscraper'.
5. Cost of re-wiring people's brains: it would have taken more millions than Heinz had to get loyal Covent Garden fans to not only try Heinz chilled soup, but keep on buying it.

After 18 months, Heinz had only been able to build a small business with £1 million in sales, minuscule compared to Covent Garden's £55 million. Early in 2009, Heinz withdrew the Farmers' Market chilled soups.

Now the flipside. Where Heinz was much more successful was in growing the core canned soup business (Figure 3.1), where Heinz is the Leader Brand. This business is the key source of profit, benefiting from decades of heritage, economies and a mastery of the business model. Canned soup is also the source of authority for Heinz and what the brand is famous for. Heinz confounded the critics of canned

Figure 3.1: Growing the core of Heinz.

soup who said it had become 'commoditised'. The company grew this business by £5 million between 2005 and 2007, to £83 million, with product upgrades, packaging design and advertising support. Five times more growth than it got from stretching into chilled soup.

So what does this mean? The Heinz story shows the big advantages that core brand growth offers:

- It doesn't create additional complexity;
- It increases economies of scale;
- It's more profitable than new products in most cases;
- It reinforces and refreshes what made you famous.

The Heinz story also shows how to avoid the trap of thinking of the core business as a commodity business with low growth potential, with the only way to grow being sexier new markets beyond the core. As Theodore Levitt famously said (1):

> There is no such thing as a commodity. Anything can be differentiated, which is precisely the marketer's job. Believing that your firm—and the services it offers – are commodities is a self-fulfilling prophecy. If you think you are a commodity, so will your customers. How could they believe otherwise? This notion of selling a commodity is a pernicious belief. It leads to price wars, incessant copying of competitors' offerings, lack of innovation, creativity, and dynamism, as well as suboptimal pricing strategies.

The case for the core

The case for growing the core is a compelling one, as shown by research done by Bain & Company (2). Bain looked at a large panel of companies and highlighted a small group of what they called 'sustained value creators' that had delivered profitable revenue growth over a 10-year period. These companies made up only 12% of those researched. They found that almost 80% of these companies had one core business in which they had a leading position. Further support for core growth comes from looking at the financial performance of company acquisitions. 'Scale deals', where a company buys another one operating in the same business, perform significantly better than 'scope deals', where the acquisition is of a company operating in a different business area.

To quote the authors:

> A strong core, coupled with focused leadership—the stronger and more focused, the better—is often at the epicentre of the most successful cases of sustained and profitable growth.

A new marketing mind-set – Scooty

We saw earlier that the risk for a core business is slow but steady decline. With the company focused on innovation to

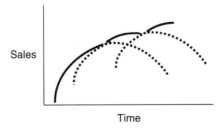

Sales

Time

Figure 3.2: Renovation waves.

stretch into new areas, the core business is left un-loved. When it does finally get some attention, it is likely to be a one-off – 'This year we're re-launching the core (then we'll get back to the real innovation).'

Growing the core requires a change in marketing mind-set. Rather than core brand growth being a one-off activity, it becomes a way of working. It involves an ongoing process of idea development and implementation to keep the core business growing. This is a bit like the ongoing 'renovation' work you need to do on a house to keep it in good order. Stretching into new markets is like building an extension to your house; however, a nice new wing for your property is not much use if your main residence is falling down! The real trick is to have 'waves' of renovation activity on the core business to keep it moving forward (Figure 3.2). Before the core business can plateau and start to decline, the next wave of activity hits the market. This wave of activity has been under development whilst the core business was still growing. In other words, you don't wait for the core business to start declining; you keep it healthy and growing. To borrow the phrase used by the French rugby coach, Bernard Laporte, 'To stay number one, you have to train like you're number two'.

Renovation waves

These waves of renovation play three important roles.

- First, they keep current users interested in the brand. They give you 'excuses for a conversation', something new and interesting to talk about.
- Second, renovation waves are an opportunity to recruit new user groups to keep the core brand growing. Every core business loses users every year, and so needs to bring in new users just to stand still.
- Third, renovation waves are a chance to respond to emerging trends and competition, keeping the brand relevant for today's consumers.

Scooty is a brand of scooters in India that targets girls and has become a distinctive and well-loved brand thanks to waves of renovation. The brand's core vision is 'to empower the expression of femininity', seeking to help women succeed in a man's world. A key way of expressing this brand vision has been through colour. Indian women enjoy wearing vibrant and cheerful colours every day, and the brand team found it odd that they had to compromise with the colour of their vehicles (you can have any colour so long as it is black . . .). Scooty's first renovation wave was offering a dramatic pink colour, a first in the auto category. Consumers lapped up this expression of their femininity. This was rapidly followed by several colour collections, taking inspiration from the fashion world. However, the ultimate renovation wave came when the brand introduced an unlimited colour choice, '99 colours', which allowed girls to express themselves in the most unique colours (Figure 3.3). This became a big hit and allowed the company to charge a premium price, as consumers were ready to pay more for a colour they felt expressed their feminine selves.

The challenges of growing the core

Even if the case for growing the core is compelling, many marketing directors find it very challenging. They face three main issues:

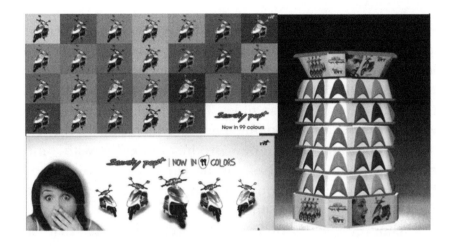

Figure 3.3: Scooty Pep+. Reproduced by permission of TVS Motor Company.

- Less sexy;
- Less well-rewarded;
- Harder to do.

Less sexy

It seems, at least at first sight, that growing the core is less sexy than brand stretching. This makes it hard sometimes to get the best marketing people excited about working on core growth, as well as getting management attention and support. After all, with brand stretching, people get to use all the toys in the marketing toy box such as product development, packaging design and new communication. In contrast, growing the core might involve no changes to the product and packaging at all.

One solution to this problem is to find good examples of core growth within the company and write these up as exciting and inspiring case studies. In addition, it may help to look for examples from companies where growing the core is seen as important work. For example, at Nike, some of the most exciting and effective marketing is not in new product launches but activations of major sports properties, such as the World Cup, and Nike's own properties, like Run London.

Less well-rewarded

There is also some feeling amongst marketing folk that launching an exciting new product or service is a better way to get promoted, as it makes more noise and, in some ways, the results are more tangible. This is made worse by the rapid turnover of marketing people which allows them to 'launch and run'. Get the new product to market with a nice big launch budget and bask in the glory. Then move onto a bigger job, leaving the poor person who takes your place to fight it out in years two and three.

Encouragingly, *brandgym* research suggests that an increasing number of companies are starting to 'see the light' and recognise how powerful core brand growth can be. It seems that the tough economic times have played a role here, with marketing directors reporting that growing the core was the best way of growing during the hard times (Figure 3.4). In addition, 98% of the panel said that core growth was a long-term change they would adopt, rather than a short-term tactic.

Senior management have a key role to play here in demonstrating their support for growing the core. We saw

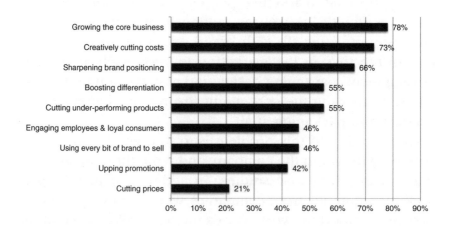

Figure 3.4: Effective techniques used to grow in recession.
(Source: *brandgym* research, June 2009).

this work well at one of our clients, a multinational food business, through the actions of one of the key-country managing directors. He required every brand presentation to begin with the team showing several of the key Grow the Core tools we had created for the business.

Harder to do

Last, and perhaps most importantly, growing the core requires as much, if not *more*, creativity than brand stretching. When you think about it, new product development has a pretty well-defined process that most marketers are trained to follow: develop and screen concepts, work with R&D on a product, brief in pack design and advertising, finalise the mix, present to retailers etc.. Of course, the road is far from easy, and getting successfully to the end is hard. But the steps to take are clear. In contrast, if you have been asked to grow the core business by 5% with no changes to product and packaging, there is much less help at hand. As mentioned already, there are more than 40 000 innovation books on Amazon.com, but none that specifically address core brand growth.

That is why the rest of this book focuses on providing practical advice and inspiration to help you grow the core:

- *Part II Grow the Core Principles*: firstly, I look at the importance of understanding what made your business famous and finding ways of keeping this fresh and relevant. Secondly, you'll discover how to get the right balance between consistency and change when growing the core.
- *Part III Grow the Core Workouts*: this programme of eight practical workouts is illustrated with brand examples to help you grow your business.
- *Part IV The Grow the Core Workplan*: this part gives practical advice on how to get started on growing your own core business, including tools, tips and tricks.

Key takeouts

1. Growing the core has several key benefits compared to brand stretch, making what is strong even stronger from both a brand and business standpoint.
2. The case for growing the core is compelling, with evidence that high-performance companies have a focus on gaining and retaining leadership in their core business.
3. Growing the core is challenging, requiring as much, or even more, creativity as brand stretching.

 Checklist 3. The case for the core

	Yes	No
• Have you found good examples of growing the core from within your business to help make a case for it?	☐	☐
• Have you also looked for inspiring examples of growing the core from other brands outside your company?	☐	☐
• Have you worked to get senior management aligned and engaged with the importance of growing the core brand?	☐	☐

 Handover

You have now seen the advantages of growing the core and how it can make what is strong even stronger, both in terms of your brand and business. You have now reached the end of Part I on Why Grow the Core? Next up in Part II of the book I look at The Grow the Core Principles, starting with the drivers you can use to grow the core.

GROW THE CORE PRINCIPLES

PART II

The core growth drivers

 Headlines

The two ways to grow the core are penetration and pre-miumisation. Driving penetration involves widening the base of users and making the brand more popular. The drivers to do this are creating a distinctive marketing mix, so the brand is recalled and relevant at the point of decision-making, and boosting distribution to make the brand available in more places. Premiumisation involves launching value-added extensions to the core offering, using both new products and new pack formats.

Having made the case for growing the core, I will now look in more detail at how to do this. First, you will see how to grow volume share by building penetration, then you will see how to drive value growth through premium extensions to the core (Figure 4.1).

Core growth driver 1: Penetration

Most marketers, myself included, have been trained to work on many ways of driving volume share growth on the core business. These include trying to boost rates of re-purchase, increase frequency of purchase and growing the amount bought on each shopping trip. A whole multi-million pound research industry has grown up to measure all these different variables in incredible detail and track them over time. Well, if you're one of the many people investing time and money on a project to drive one of these variables, at this point you might want to grab a cup of tea or something even stronger, as you're in for a shock.

In my case, the shock came at an event organised by the IPA in London, where Professor Byron Sharp of The Ehrenberg-Bass Institute (EIB) was promoting his book, *How Brands Grow* (1). Byron was presenting his 'scientific laws of marketing', which are the fruit of many years of scientific research covering multiple categories and markets, across both business-to-business and business-to-consumer categories.

So, what's the shock? Byron and his team show convincingly that the only way to grow volume share is by increasing penetration to expand the base of people using your brand. Your brand's user base includes a mix of light, medium and heavy buyers. But the mix of these loyalty levels is likely to be similar to that of other brands in your category. Indeed, Byron's work shows that the most important group for growth is not the loyal users who buy your brand frequently. This group contains 'brand fans' who know you well and are likely to carry on buying you. No, the key groups for growth are the many light and non-users who are on the verge of buying you or another brand at some point in the year. There are a lot of these 'floating voters' who can swing towards your brand or the competition. In his book, Byron gives the example of Coca-Cola, a brand you would think is bought very frequently. In reality, over half of the UK buyers of Coca-Cola buy it only once or twice a year. The main role of marketing is to ensure that when one of these people is deciding what to buy, they choose you and not another brand.

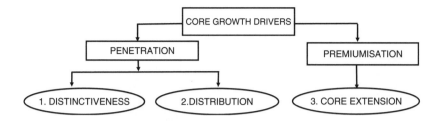

Figure 4.1: Core brand growth drivers.

'What about increasing loyalty?' you may reply. Well, Byron blows to bits the concept of loyalty using the law of 'double jeopardy'. This law was discovered by Professor Andrew Ehrenberg, founder of the EIB. It shows that within a given category all brands have similar levels of loyalty. The only difference is that the bigger brands with higher penetration enjoy slightly higher loyalty levels. In other words, you can have some impact on loyalty, but only by increasing your penetration level!

Still not convinced? Let's quickly look at some examples to illustrate the importance of penetration. Feel free to skip this next bit if you are sold on penetration being the way to grow volume share.

Penetration drives volume share

First, here's an example from consumer goods based on the US shampoo market (Figure 4.2) featured in Byron's book. We can see straight away that volume share increases in line with penetration. The biggest brand by volume, Suave, has the highest level of penetration. It has a bigger group of people using it at least once in the past year. In contrast, the levels of loyalty are quite similar, as measured by annual purchase frequency. We also see that Suave has a slightly higher level of loyalty, in line with its higher penetration, in line with the law of double jeopardy.

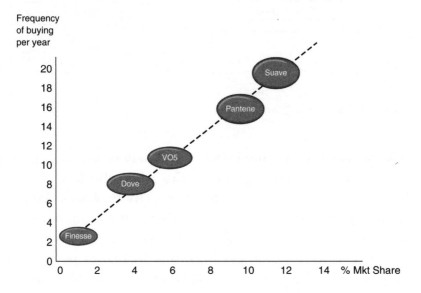

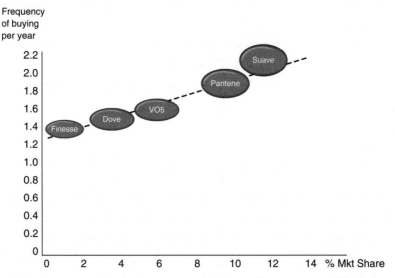

Figure 4.2: Penetration and loyalty vs. market share in US shampoo market in 2005.

(Source: *How Brands Grow*, by Byron Sharp).

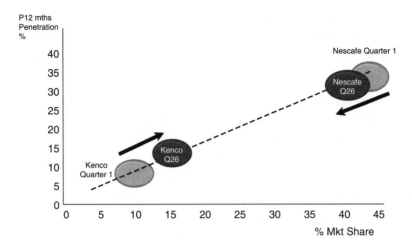

Figure 4.3: Changes in UK coffee market share are driven by penetration.
(Source: TNS analysis by Charles Graham).

Now, you could argue these data are only a snapshot in time. They show what makes one brand bigger than another, but don't actually show how brands grow over time. Another study done by research agency TNS helps show that growth over time also reflects changes in penetration (2). You can see from Figure 4.3 how the increase in share of Kenco reflects an increase in penetration, whilst the drop in share of Nescafé is linked to a drop in penetration.

What about service brands, they might be different, right? In fact, the same story applies. Looking at data for super-markets, we see the same pattern. Tesco is the UK's biggest supermarket thanks to a higher level of penetration (3). The law of double jeopardy applies again, with Tesco also enjoy-ing a higher level of loyalty, as measured by share of buying requirements.

The exception of category growth

An important point to remember here is that all of the above findings on penetration being the way to grow volume share apply to *a given category*. Loyalty and frequency rates may differ between categories, and between the same category in different markets. For example, people in the USA drink a lot more cola than those in the UK. Indeed, Coca-Cola uses 'consumption per capita' as a key measure to look at the potential to get certain countries guzzling more fizzy drinks. However, in the more developed US soft drinks market, all brands benefit from the higher frequency.

This means that one additional way to grow volume is to drive category growth. The issue here is that you will not only be driving growth of the category as a whole for the benefit of your brand, but also all your competitors! This is why this strategy only makes sense if you are a dominant leader in the category. For example, Gillette's promotion of all-over-body shaving for men could work well given that the brand has a 75%+ share of the shaving market.

So, having seen that to grow the core you need to drive penetration and widen your user base, I'll show you how to do this, starting with distinctive marketing and then covering distribution.

Driving penetration with distinctiveness

As we saw earlier, the most important group for driving penetration and growing volume share is the large number of floating voters: light and non-users. The first way to get as many of these people as possible to buy your brand is to increase brand 'saliency', so you are recalled and relevant when they do decide to buy your category.

Distinctiveness not differentiation

Now, the best way to be recalled and relevant is to differentiate, right? After all, as one of the world's foremost marketing strategists, Jack Trout, writes in his seminal book, we have one of two choices: 'Differentiate or Die'. In fact,

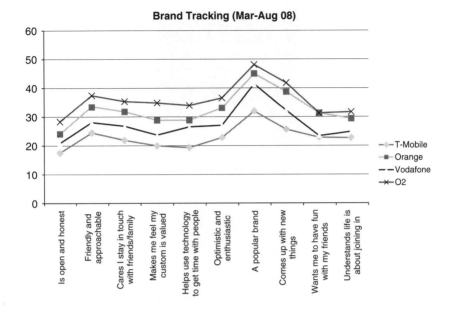

Figure 4.4: Brands with similar image profiles.

differentiation will seriously limit your potential to grow the core. Differentiation will drive you to seek out secondary benefits. In doing so, you risk reducing your appeal, as you have moved away from the middle-ground of the market and the most important core benefits people want.

Leader Brands are, in fact, not differentiated, as an example from brand image tracking in the UK mobile network market shows in Figure 4.4. O₂ is the Leader Brand and it's not differentiated. The brand doesn't stand out for one thing in particular. Rather, O₂ is stronger across the board. It has a similar image *profile* to smaller brands like Orange and T-Mobile, as you can see. The shape of the O₂ image graph is the same as the other brands, it's just higher on everything. Instead of searching for *differentiation* through unique benefits, which would take them away from the heart of what people want, Leader Brands like O₂ create highly *distinctive* marketing mixes. This allows them to express the core market

Figure 4.5: Distinctive brand world.

benefits in a way that is more impactful and memorable. O_2 uses a highly impactful blue and bubbly visual brand world to stand out (Figure 4.5). Being first to market with products like the iPhone has enhanced its image for innovation. The O_2 Rewards scheme helped communicate customer care (interestingly, this was set up as a loyalty scheme, but actually worked by increasing penetration and attracting new users who thought, 'O_2 seems to care about its customers, I'll give them a go').

In summary, to grow the core, distinctiveness is more important than differentiation.

Memory matters

To further explore how distinctive marketing can help grow the core, think back to your last trip to the supermarket (thanks to Andy Knowles from JKR for this story). If you're an average shopper, you would have bought around 30 items. If it was an average supermarket, you had 30 000 items to choose from. In other words, for each thing you bought, you chose 1 in 1000 of the items on sale. And you left 999 on the shelf:

- Average number of items in a supermarket = 30 000
- Average number of items in shopping basket = 30
- For each item bought, number of things you DO buy = 1 in 1000
- For each item bought, number of things you DON'T buy = 999 out of 1000

Now, how long did it take you to do this incredibly difficult task? Again, if you're an average shopper, it probably took you about 30 minutes. But how is this possible? How can you make a 1 in 1000 choice, 30 times over, in only 30 minutes?

The answer can be found by understanding how our brains work. For 90% of the time they work on 'auto-pilot' in order to conserve energy and not burn out. You act without actually thinking. This auto-pilot behaviour happens using 'memory structure': hard-wired associations linked to distinctive symbols, slogans and other 'brand properties'. The distinctive brand properties that are key to creating memory structure can take many forms, such as Marlboro's use of the colour red, Nike's swoosh symbol and Coca-Cola's script typeface.

So, when we see a red light we just stop, and when the light turns green, we go. In the same way, when shopping, we make most of our decisions on auto-pilot using memory structure. A commuter passes the news-stand and sees the salmon colour of the *Financial Times* and picks it up without thinking. In the supermarket you see a red can with a white swoosh and, without thinking, a six-pack of Coca-Cola is in your shopping trolley. On a minority of occasions we will stop, perhaps to review prices or promotions. Here, we actually engage our brains and think, but most of the time we draw on memory structure to decide what to buy. This is why distinctiveness is so important in helping increase penetration and to grow the core.

The same situation applies in the online world. Again, we are bombarded with brand choices. The way our brains cope with this is to use memory structure to simplify the choice process. This is one of the reasons for shopping comparison websites to invest in building distinctive brand properties linked to their website addresses, such as the meerkat character of Compare the Market and the opera singer of Go Compare in the UK.

Fresh consistency – James Bond

Neuro-science research suggests that this memory structure takes two to three years to establish (4). For an insight into why many brands fail to create a lot of memory structure, look no further than the average tenure of a marketing director: two and a half years. A new marketing director's arrival is often the trigger for a change of agency and communication campaign, just at the point that the previous campaign was about to establish some memory structure! Part of the problem here is that marketing people seem to get bored more easily than consumers and so change their marketing more often than is really needed in the search for novelty.

Creating distinctiveness to drive penetration of the core requires a skilful balancing act between consistency and change (Figure 4.6), or 'fresh consistency' for short (thanks to Charlie Hiscox at SAB Miller for this term). On the one side, there is a need to look forward to new trends and keep the brand fresh to stay relevant. Most companies seem to spend a lot of time and money doing this. However, where many companies miss a trick is balancing freshness with some consistency. As we saw earlier, the consistent use of brand properties is key to creating the memory structure that helps brands get recalled and onto the shopping list. This

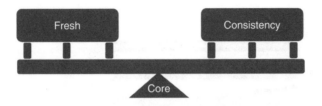

Figure 4.6: The core brand balancing act.

is why it's important to also look back and remember what made the brand famous. Yet, on Grow the Core projects, a simple request for a 15–20 year reel of advertising leaves many brand teams flummoxed. Often, the response is 'I've worked here for two years and can go back that far. Before that, I'm not sure.' Even when a commercial reel is produced, watching it is often like seeing four or five different brands. Campaigns zig and zag all over the place, and you can often link these changes to the all-too-frequent arrival of a new marketing director. This sort of inconsistency can confuse rather than convince consumers. What the brand stands for becomes diluted and there is a failure to create, amplify and reinforce brand properties to build memory structure.

One brand that has done a great job of remembering and refreshing what made it famous is Bond, James Bond. To borrow a phrase from one of the Bond theme tunes, 'Nobody does it better' when it comes to fresh consistency. For more than 40 years brand Bond has gone through a series of updates, linked to the arrival of new actors in the starring role, and this process of constant renovation has been able to keep the box office tills ringing ever louder (5), as Figure 4.7 shows. It's interesting to see the 'bump' that occurs with the introduction of each new Bond.

The most recent renovation happened with the twenty-first Bond movie, *Casino Royale*. This featured a new actor in the starring role, Daniel Craig. The movie smashed all box office records for the Bond franchise and the opening UK

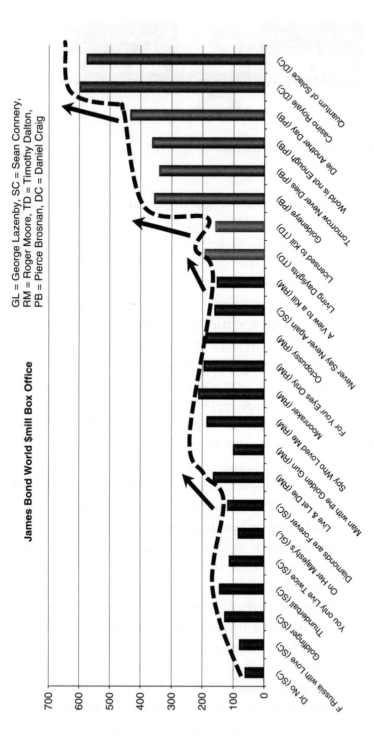

Figure 4.7: Renovation of brand Bond through new Bond actors.

(Source: Wikipedia).

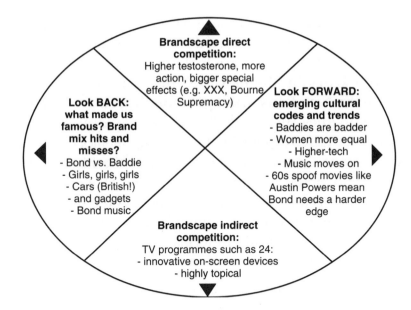

Figure 4.8: Looking back, looking forward for James Bond.

weekend box-office takings of £13 million were up 40% on the previous high for *Die Another Day*. This was followed up by another hit with *Quantum of Solace*. Forty-four years after the first Bond movie came out, the brand is still going strong.

Looking at the enduring success of the Bond brand, we can see at least four things that the producers have taken into account (Figure 4.8):

- **Looking back:** at what made Bond famous.
- **Looking forward:** at how the world is changing.
- **Direct competition:** from other film franchises that could steal attention from Bond.
- **Indirect competition:** from new forms of competition out there.

Looking back

Looking back at what made you famous is a bit like 'brand archaeology'. You dig into your past marketing mix and look for hidden treasure. When was the brand 'hot', growing share and sales, and when was it 'cold'? What was the brand doing at these times? Here, you are looking for two things. Firstly, you are looking at 'the message': the content of the brand promise the brand was making. Secondly, you are looking at brand properties such as endlines, creative ideas and visual devices that were responsible for creating memory structure.

We can use this approach and look at the history of the James Bond brand. There are a number of elements that have been constant over time. First, there is the fundamental 'brand idea' which could be summarised as 'Bond beats the baddie to save the world'. In terms of brand properties, the list goes on and on and includes:

- **The gorgeous girls**, at least one of whom is actually up to no good.
- **The car** that goes fast but also has loads of gadgets.
- **The music:** dang dang-a-lang-lang... dang dang dang dang dang-a-lang-lang... dang dang dang dang da da, da da da etc.
- **The catchphrases:** 'Bond; James Bond. 'Martini, shaken not stirred.'.
- **The characters:** Q, M, Miss Moneypenny.

Looking forward

At the same time as rewinding to look at what made your brand famous in the past and what built its strong brand associations, there is also a need to look to the future and how the world is changing. For James Bond relevant trends might include the rise of global terrorism, with baddies getting badder, and the changing role of women.

Direct and indirect competition

Bond's direct competition is getting tougher, with the emergence of other action hero movies, especially the Bourne

JAMES BOND

KEEP = Consistency	UPDATE = Freshness	LOSE = Freshness	ADD = Freshness
• Central idea of 'Bond vs. Baddie to save the world' • Core elements of the character: cars, girls, gadgets • Theme tune and 007 id	• Core elements such as cars and gadgets need to be higher-tech • Baddies need to be badder • Update music and id	• Foreign influences: e.g. cars should be British!	• References to current affairs and events

Figure 4.9: Highlighting fresh consistency.

series. It's also important to consider 'indirect' competition: brands operating in different markets which can potentially steal business from you. This is often where new competition, such as Kodak losing out to Samsung and Sony as the photography market moved from film to digital, can catch out long-established brands. In the case of James Bond, indirect competition could include TV programmes like *24*, with its high-tech feel and imperfect hard-edged hero Jack Bauer.

Finding fresh consistency

After looking back, forward and at the competition, the next task is to decide on which elements need keeping, updating, losing and adding (Figure 4.9). This is key to creating fresh consistency and so building and reinforcing memory structure.

Bottle the magic

Having done the James Bond exercise to look back and look forward, it's important to check you have a clear and inspiring vision for your brand. I call this 'bottling the magic'. This means understanding what the brand stands for today and, more importantly, having a vision of what you want it to

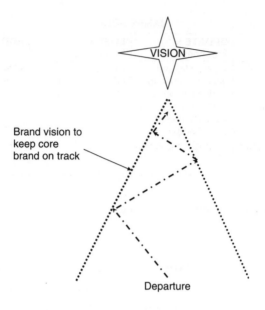

Figure 4.10: GPS for core brand.

stand for in the future. When brands are struggling to grow the core, this often reflects the lack of clear brand vision that the whole business has bought into. In these cases there is lots of activity, as different bits of the business run around searching for short-term sources of sales. In fact, there is too much activity, heading off in different directions and so fragmenting investment, time and talent.

When you have a clear vision, it works in two ways to help you grow the core. First, a good vision inspires ideas and creativity. Second, the vision keeps the whole team on track to the desired destination in the same way a GPS system works in a car (Figure 4.10).

The process and tools for creating a brand vision are discussed in detail in an earlier *brandgym* book, *Brand Vision: How to energize your team to drive business growth*. Here, I will just do a quick review of the two key components of a brand vision: the 'recipe' and the 'cake'.

Recipe: brand positioning tool

The detailed recipe for your brand vision can be captured in a brand positioning tool. These come in many different shapes and sizes. But when you strip away the sales talk promoting the latest fancy tool, they're all basically the same. The most important bit is the content. The tool we normally use on *brandgym* projects is shown in Figure 4.11, with an example for the Pampers brand. This captures the re-positioning of the brand from a very rational and problem-focused brand into a supportive ally for parents. This new vision for Pampers inspired and guided growth on the core diaper business, with market share up strongly from 47% to 55% in the 18 months following the re-launch. For example, 'New Baby' diapers were specially developed for (ugh!) runny poo that comes from a liquid diet. 'Active Fit' has extra stretchy

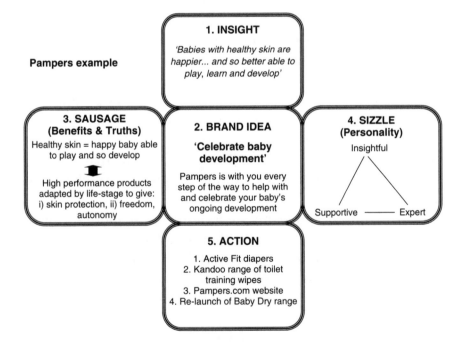

Figure 4.11: Brand vision tool for Pampers.
(Source: author's own).

sides to provide a perfect fit when the baby is older and on the move.

Cake: inspiration

Once you have the detailed brand positioning, you then also need to bring it to life. After all, standing up and showing people your brand pyramid or onion is a bit like Gordon Ramsay coming to the dinner table and presenting his guests with a detailed recipe of the cake they are about to eat. All you care about is what the cake looks like and how it tastes. The same thing goes for brands: you need to 'sell the cake, not the recipe'. In this case, the cake is the brand mix, so you need to bring to life the brand story in a visual way.

For example, the global brand team at Hellmann's created a food magazine to communicate their new vision about making casual eating more pleasurable by adding exciting tastes and textures. This was much more effective than a traditional, big fat brand book in a binder. The Hellmann's brand vision was written as a 'story' using everyday language, not jargon (Table 4.1). For example, the 'core consumer profile' was told using a diary of a week in the life of a typical consumer called Katherine. Instead of talking about 'benefits' and 'reasons to believe' the presentation asked 'How can we help Katherine?' and 'Why should she believe us'. Most important of all, there was a page on 'The story so far' that showed examples of product, packs and events that were closest to the desired vision.

Increasingly, brand teams are looking to use more sophisticated visual aids to bring to life their visions, especially video. For example, Shell Retail produced a TV soap opera to show the contrasting fortunes of one store managed in line with the brand vision and another that was stuck in the past. The trick with brand videos is to ensure that the video tells a brand story with the help of visuals and music. It helps to use wording on the screen at key moments to show the key phrases from the brand vision, and the video should be no

Table 4.1: Selling the cake not the recipe

Traditional brand book	Hellmann's magazine	Visuals used
Contents	'Menu du jour'	Waiter and menu board
Root strengths	Back to the future	Restaurant counter with natural ingredients
Target audience	A week in the life of Katherine	Diary with photos
Benefits	What can we do for Katherine?	Simple visual of the 3 key benefits
Reasons to believe	Why should Katherine believe us?	Visuals of packs and products that support the benefits
Strategic plan	To do list	Handwritten list of things to do stuck to a fridge door

longer than one to two minutes. The thing to avoid is what I call 'MTV videos' that just have a sequence of exciting visuals and a nice rock-music track, but don't really communicate the vision. With a good brand video you should be able to play it for a new brand team member or agency and at the end have them understanding 80–90% of your brand vision.

Driving penetration with distribution

Distribution certainly isn't the sexiest part of marketing, far from it. There are conferences aplenty on the red-hot topic of social media at the moment. Try and find a conference on increasing distribution and you'll struggle. However, whilst no one has proven that terrific Tweeting or fabulous Facebook pages will grow your core, I'd bet my life-savings that your product being sold in more places will help you sell more stuff. Distribution gets your brand in front of as many people as possible, including that important group of light and non-users we have been talking about. Simply put, if your brand is not available at the moment when these floating voters decide what to buy, then you've missed your chance to build the penetration of the core.

At the simplest level, distribution is about making your brand available in existing channels. So, for a typical consumer goods brand, this means maximising presence in the major supermarkets.

Distribution is also about looking at new 'routes to the consumer' by opening up new channels. This could be selling your brand in places where the product is not normally sold, such as the Calvin Klein CK1 fragrance selling in fashion stores. Or, it could be finding a way to sell direct to the consumer, such as Apple building its own chain of retail stores.

Core growth driver 2: Premiumisation

The driver of increasing penetration focuses on growing *volume* share. The second core growth driver is premiumisation: making more money for each bit of volume you sell and growing *value* share. This can be achieved by significantly upgrading the existing product or service to support a higher price. However, more often it will involve delivering new versions of the core that add extra value to consumers and so can be sold at a premium price. As long as the percentage profit of the core extension is the same as the original version, this means extra cash profit per unit sold. Even if the new product 'cannibalises' volume from the existing products, overall profit will go up.

Core extension can be done through offering a new product, such as Ryvita crispbreads launching versions with seeds offering both health benefits and a more interesting taste experience. It can also come through different pack formats, such as Heinz selling its ketchup in an upside-down, squeezy bottle that's easier to use than the original glass one.

The key point here is adding value. Many brand extensions fail to offer new and relevant benefits to consumers and so fail in the marketplace. Another common problem is where a company dreams up a new product that is more expensive to make, but doesn't offer enough value to consumers to be sold at a sufficient premium to maintain profitability.

The Grow the Core workouts

There are eight workouts in the *brandgym* Grow the Core programme (Figure 4.12). The sequence of the workouts is important, in that the first six involve working with the existing core product or service to sell more stuff, 'SMS' for short. This form of core growth is incredibly potent as it increases sales without adding any extra complexity. The result is making what is strong even stronger and so driving economies of scale.

Only after working through the first six SMS workouts do we move on to extending the core and creating additional products and pack formats. These do add complexity, hence our focus on ensuring these extensions add value and so justify a premium price.

Here we give a quick introduction to the six drivers covered by the workouts, each of which then has a chapter of its own to go into more detail.

1. *Product:* the strongest brands don't rely on communication to grow. Rather they 'bake the brand' into the product or service to make it distinctive.
2. *Identity:* brand identity is at the heart of creating a more distinctive mix. In particular, you will see the power of brand properties to build memory structure. These brand properties can be used in packaging design, but the strongest ones are amplified across the whole of the mix.
3. *Communication:* communication can be a highly effective driver of core growth when the focus is on distinctiveness that helps the brand be recalled and relevant at the point of buying. Here I will cover not only classic media like TV, but also the hot topic of

Figure 4.12: Core brand growth drivers.

social media and the role they can play in helping you SMS.

4. *Activation:* much of the money spent on promotions drives short-term spikes in sales (followed by dips in sales) but does little to create memory structure. I will explain how to create activation properties which are more effective at making the brand distinctive.

5. and 6. *Distribution:* in existing channels there is much that can be done to increase availability. It might not be as sexy as social media, but getting your brand into more places is a much more reliable way of selling more stuff. Given the increasing power

of the major retailers, the most innovative brands are looking to create new 'routes to the consumer' which allow more control over how the brand is marketed, whilst driving increased penetration.

7. and 8. *Core extension:* the first way of premiumising the brand is to create new products which add value to the core by adding new benefits or by addressing barriers to trial of the current offering. Pack innovation via new formats can also be an excellent way of boosting both penetration and profitability.

The best brand in the world – Nespresso?

Having introduced the eight key drivers of core brand growth, we'll look at an example of how these can be used on what I consider to be 'the best brand in the world': Nespresso. This is a 'system brand', based on coffee machines made with partners such as Krupps which use Nespresso capsules (Figure 4.13). Senseo, Tassimo and Nestlé's own Dolce Gusto are also competing for a share of this coffee 'pod' market. But Nespresso is the leader in the premium segment.

Figure 4.13: The best brand in the world.

To get an idea how clever the total system is, the concept (machine, capsule, service) is subject to 1700 patents. And with $2.5 billion in sales, this is now one of the biggest consumer goods brands in the world. It has also achieved an eye-popping growth rate, growing at an average of 30% a year in the nine years from 2000 to 2009. Let's have a look at how it has used each of the core growth drivers:

- distinctiveness, via product, identity and communication;
- distribution;
- core extension.

Distinctive product

At the heart of Nespresso is a fantastic product experience. A huge amount of research went into creating the system and, in particular, delivering the 'crema' topping you get on a real espresso. Now, get this. Nestlé researchers first designed the capsule in 1970 and the brand was launched in ... 1986. So, 16 years of research and development.

The company is incredibly selective in the coffee it uses, effectively selecting beans from the best 1% of the worldwide crop. The range of 16 *grands crus* coffees with exotic names also makes it distinctive from the more conventionally presented competition.

Nespresso has made significant progress on sourcing, working for six years with the Rainforest Alliance on 'AAA' coffee, which is of the highest quality but also environmentally sustainable and beneficial to farmers. This is a hell of a task, as the brand can't compromise on quality. Already 50% of all the coffee sold is AAA and the brand is on track to have achieved 80% by 2013, which is pretty damn good. The area where Nespresso does get some stick is on the environmental impact of the capsules, but even here the brand is not sitting back. The good news is that the aluminium the pods are made of is infinitely recyclable and the brand has now developed capsule retrieval systems in France, Switzerland, Portugal and Austria. By 2013 it will have tripled this network so that it has a capacity to recycle 75% of all the capsules sold.

Distinctive identity

The coffee is sold in beautiful little capsules, with different colours for different tastes. The capsules are highly distinctive, with each one looking almost like a piece of jewellery. They also create a highly impactful display when merchandised in the Nespresso boutiques. You can buy one of a range of machines, which in themselves are design objects.

Distinctive communication

The brand has delivered a product story in a distinctive way through a consistently executed communication campaign starring George Clooney. The star has been used to endorse the brand since 2005, adding emotional appeal and reinforcing the brand's premiumness. This means Clooney has become a real brand property, quite an achievement given that he does adverts for several brands. The endorsement is credible, as you do believe he is the sort of guy who would drink Nespresso. There has also been consistent use of the same endline, 'Nespresso. What else?', again helping to create distinctive memory structure. A final bit of memory structure is the Nespresso boutique, which is always featured in communication. What's great here is that you can actually go to one of the boutiques for yourself.

The brand has also been smart in injecting freshness into the campaign by telling a series of different stories featuring the star. Early adverts were quite straightforward. For example, in one, George meets beautiful Brazilian actress Camilla Belle and thinks she wants his autograph, but in fact it's the Nespresso she wants. More recent adverts are mini-movie masterpieces, starring George and John Malkovich.

Here, Clooney gets hit by a piano leaving the Nespresso boutique and goes to heaven. At the gates to heaven he meets Malkovich who offers him the chance to return to his life on Earth ... in exchange for his Nespresso. The casting, direction and aesthetic are excellent and the product is the star of the story.

Distribution

At the heart of Nespresso's stunning success is a different distribution model to your average consumer goods brand. Unlike most brands, Nespresso is not in a death-match with retailers. Instead, it sells coffee through three routes to consumer:

- Online: via a very efficient website which remembers what you ordered last time, allowing you to quickly re-order.
- Boutiques: for people who like personal service and want to check out new launches.
- Telephone: for people who want to order from home, but want to talk to someone.

All of these routes to consumer are 100% controlled by the brand, which delivers a whole host of benefits that most marketing directors can only dream of:

- 100% distribution.
- Perfect display.
- Guaranteed, instant and controlled launch of new products.
- Total control over promotions.
- Two-way customer dialogue: Nespresso has several million 'members' of the Nespresso club, allowing a dialogue with them to propose new ideas, track what they buy and ask for feedback. It can measure performance in real time, rather than having to pay the retailer to get these data.

This business model is hard to copy. Nespresso has been at this for 24 years, building up expertise, systems and highly trained staff.

Core extension

Nespresso has also extended the core in several directions to further boost penetration. First, the brand has extended beyond the espresso versions most associated with premium coffee to offer a range of 'Lungo' long coffees. These are important for some markets such as the USA and UK. Second, the brand makes excellent use of limited edition products to add distinctiveness and keep the brand fresh and interesting. These include seasonal products based on taste-related themes, such as Onirio in 2011, which had 'white floral notes, reminiscent of jasmine and orange blossom, followed by roasted notes.' In addition, the brand offers a series of seasonal 'Editions' products at Christmas, such as Vanilla Blossom, Cherry and Dark Chocolate in 2011.

The Nespresso story has hopefully whetted your appetite for knowledge about how to grow the core, giving you a taste for the eight growth drivers. As you read on, I will go into more detail about each of the drivers.

 Key takeouts

1. The two key ways to grow the core are penetration (volume) and premiumisation (value).
2. Increased penetration comes through distinctive marketing to establish memory structure and by growing distribution.
3. Premiumisation is delivered by added value products and pack formats.

Checklist 4. Core growth drivers

	Yes	No
• Have you got data from your own business to show how market share correlates with penetration?	☐	☐
• Have you done the 'Brand Bond' exercise to look back at what made you famous, and what the future trends are?	☐	☐
• Do you have a clear view on the key brand properties you will use to create fresh consistency?	☐	☐
• Have your brought to life your brand vision to inspire and guide core growth?	☐	☐

 ## Handover

We have now introduced the two key drivers to grow the core: penetration and premiumisation, and we have had an overview of the eight workouts that make up the Grow the Core programme. Before looking at each workout in depth, we need to understand the balance between freshness and consistency, which depends on the health of the brand and the market in which it operates.

Renovation or re-invention?

CHAPTER 5

 Headlines

The growth strategy to adopt on the core business depends on the health of the brand and also the market in which the core business is operating. If the brand and market are relatively healthy, then the best approach is an ongoing programme of renovation. If the brand is stagnant or in long-term decline, re-positioning of the core may be needed, though this is harder to pull off. At the other extreme is a core business where the whole market is threatened by disruptive technology, requiring a more radical and risky re-invention of the core.

An important step before starting work on growing the core is to assess the health of the core brand and business. The results of this work will guide the balance between the freshness and consistency that is needed to grow the core, as we saw in the last chapter. Without this important step, companies can rush into a programme of work, running the risk of either changing too much or not enough.

Most companies today have a way of measuring brand health, using a combination of business measures (market share, revenue growth, profitability) and brand equity measures (awareness, brand image attributes, consumer satisfaction). You also need to look at the category in

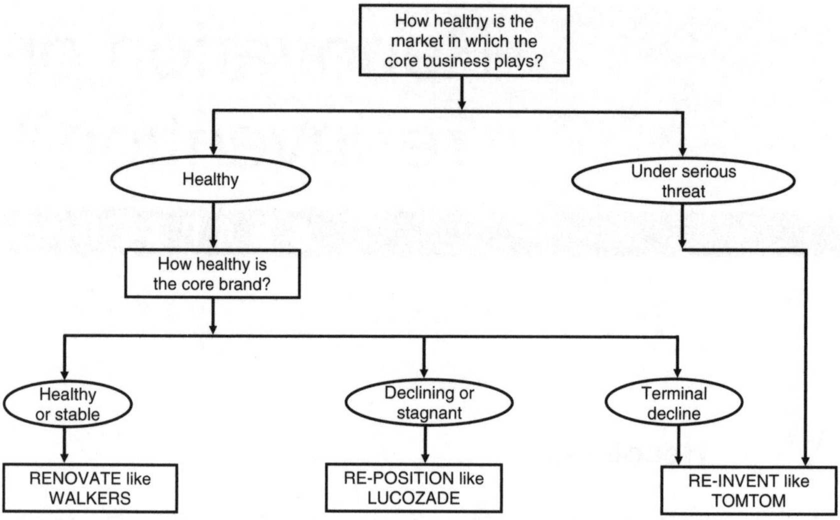

Figure 5.1: Core brand health check to guide growth strategy.

which the brand is operating in terms of size, growth and profitability.

To keep things simple, I will cover four main types of challenge on the core business that come out of a core brand health check, starting with the healthiest brand and ending with the least healthy (Figure 5.1):

• Core brand renovation: in this ideal case, the market in which the brand operates is relatively healthy. And the brand itself is also in good health. The challenge here is to continue to keep the brand fresh with integrated chapters of 'news' such as product upgrade, packaging improvement and activation, whilst keeping consistency of brand story and brand properties. To illustrate this approach we will look at Walkers, the UK's leading potato chip brand, which has used a communication campaign featuring a famous footballer to support multiple chapters of activity for more than 16 years.
• Re-positioning: in this case, the market in which the brand competes is again in relatively good health. However, the

brand is stagnant or even in decline. More freshness is needed to re-position the brand to deliver new benefits, or to target new users and/or occasions. We will look at the story of Lucozade, a drink that was used as a sickness remedy and that was successfully re-positioned as an energy drink.

- Re-define: this case is where the original core business has become unattractive, perhaps because it is unprofitable. There may be an opportunity to re-define the core, but focusing on another part of the business which brings to life the brand and has more potential for profitable growth. We will look at how the Bertolli brand re-defined its core.
- Re-invention: this is the most challenging case of all. In this case, the market in which the brand operates is in sharp or even terminal decline. The underlying core benefit the brand offers might still be relevant. However, to survive, the brand needs a totally fresh way of delivering the core benefit. To illustrate this approach we will look at the example of the Kodak brand trying to come to grips with the challenges of digital photography.

Renovate the core – Walkers

If you're in the fortunate situation of having a core business that is stable or even growing, then the right approach is brand renovation. For most companies, core brand renovation requires a change in marketing mind-set. These companies tend to see growing the core as a punctual activity, 'This quarter we're re-launching the core. Then we'll get back to some real innovation'. However, core brand renovation involves an ongoing process of idea development and implementation to keep the core business growing.

Core renovation is a bit like staying in shape by going to the gym on a regular basis and eating a healthy diet. This way you avoid the need for drastic action such as a crash diet, or even worse, getting into more serious health problems. As discussed earlier, we need 'waves' of renovation activity on the core business to keep it moving forward. Before the core business can plateau and start to decline, the next wave of activity hits the market.

The Walkers crisps story (the brand is sold as Lays potato chips in the USA and other markets outside the UK) is a great example of a brand maintaining a healthy core business with an ongoing stream of renovation. The key branded challenger to Walkers, Golden Wonder, eventually threw in the towel and went bankrupt, finding it impossible to compete effectively. The power of the Walkers renovation mix has been a potent combination of communication and product innovation.

A rare species: a true communication campaign

The growth of the Walkers brand started back in the late 1980s when the Pepsico-owned brand merged with the local Smith's crisps business. Until then, Walkers had been a regional rather than national brand. The company created a vision for the brand around the idea of 'irresistibility' and, more specifically, 'so fantastic you'd do anything to get them'. The personality of the brand was a 'home-town boy made good'. An English football player called Gary Lineker was used to bring to life the personality in the visioning tool used. He had been famous for being a talented sportsman but also one who was very fair, having never received a red card (the most serious sanction) in his career. In what turned out to be an inspired decision, the brand team and agency decided to use the player himself as the star of the brand's advertising campaign, called 'No more Mr Nice Guy'.

The first commercial showed the player going back to his hometown and being warmly greeted by the townsfolk as their favourite son. He then sits down next to a little boy eating a packet of Walkers and proceeds to grab the crisps away from him and munch them, leaving the poor boy in tears.

Lineker has gone on to star in no less than 70 commercials over 16 years that have remained incredibly consistent to the original idea, a rare example of a brand sticking to its vision over the long run.

Wave after wave of core brand renovation

What is most impressive about Walkers is the way it has stuck loyally to its core product of potato chips and has not been tempted to head-off on brand ego trips. However, there has been no shortage of innovation over the last 15 years. In fact, there has been wave after wave of new ideas on the core business:

- **Packaging**: foil-wrapped packs that use nitrogen filling enabled the brand to deliver even fresher, crunchier crisps.
- **Healthier versions**: core range extensions to address health issues have included Lites, made with sunflower oil, and more recently Mr Potato Head low-fat crisps for kids.
- **Core upgrade on health**: the brand has gradually reduced the amount of saturated fat in the product, doing it like this to avoid people noticing the change in taste and possibly leaving the brand. After a couple of years of doing this, the brand made an on-pack claim of '70% less saturated fat, still great taste'.
- **Core upgrade on taste**: on a regular basis the brand will re-launch core flavours, such as 'now even better cheese and onion flavour'.
- **Grab bags**: bigger-size bags for bigger appetites.
- **Special flavours**: limited edition flavours such as Heinz Tomato Ketchup (sorry, this is the UK) and another linked into a bi-annual charity event called Red Nose Day.
- **Premiumisation**: the launch of the Sensations sub-brand took Walkers into premium crisps with sophisticated flavours. This generated extra sales of over £50 million.

Figure 5.2: Renovating the core in action.

- **Provenance**: most recently Walkers has been promoting the core range by communicating on the pack the use of British potatoes, tapping into a growing interest in the provenance of food products (Figure 5.2).

Re-position the core – Lucozade

If the core brand is in decline, or stagnant with few signs of growth, then a more radical approach may be needed to re-position the brand. This involves fundamentally changing one or more of the following on the core business:

- Who: the target audience;
- When: usage occasion;
- Why: key benefit.

This is much harder to do than renovation, and the chances of success are slim. This is because our perceptions of brands are 'hard-wired' into our brains and so very difficult to change. Re-positioning a brand requires a visible and significant change in the brand's behaviour and sustained investment to communicate the change.

Indeed, to show just how hard re-positioning is to do, my best example is still one from many years ago – the Lucozade brand. This is a carbonated, glucose drink that started out life in 1938 as a sickness remedy. The glucose is in a form that can be easily assimilated by the body, making it suitable for people who are ill and cannot eat properly. It was sold in supermarkets in large glass bottles covered in yellow cellophane. Any readers from the UK may remember sick days off school that were spent in bed drinking glasses of the sticky, orange liquid. However, the brand was an irregular, 'distress purchase' and as sickness levels lowered with an improved health service, sales began to decline, dropping by 30% between 1974 and 1978.

Step 1: everyday pick-me-up

The first re-visioning came in 1978 and positioned Lucozade as a healthy, daily pick-me-up, in an attempt to break out of the straitjacket of being a sickness remedy and 'distress purchase'. The re-launch relied on communication, with a cartoon execution showing a lady doing the cleaning that took her over a series of hand-drawn hills and troughs until she collapsed, exhausted, on a chair. Lucozade came to the rescue and she was off again with the next bit of housework (this was the 1970s remember) to the tune of a catchy jingle: *'Lucozade refreshes you through the ups and downs of the day'*. This re-launch was initially successful, increasing sales by 11%. However, by the end of 1979 sales growth had flattened off (1).

Step 2: a pioneer in energy drinks

The 'ups and downs of the day' re-launch had limited impact because it left the product and packaging untouched. The big bottle with the yellow cellophane remained and this still cued images of a sickness remedy, no matter how hard the advertising tried to send a different message.

The real breakthrough came from challenging the *whole* of the mix, not just the communication. The result was that Lucozade became the first 'energy drink' in the UK and one of the first in the world. The brand's user base was dramatically shifted, attracting younger drinkers buying the brand for themselves. The one thing that didn't change was the product itself, but pretty much everything else was re-invented:

- **Bottle**: a key change was to re-package the product in a smaller 250 ml, wide-mouth, hand-held bottle and get rid of the yellow cellophane. This sounds simple but it had a radical effect on the perception of the brand. The brand was now a drink to be consumed on the go, not just at home. It looked much more modern and contemporary and had thrown off its sickness remedy baggage.
- **Distribution**: the brand was expanded out of supermarkets into the thousands of small corner stores in the UK called 'CTNs' (confectioners, tobacconists and newsagents). These are stores where kids from school stop off and buy drinks and snacks on the way home. Lucozade was now available in this outlet as a great option for getting an energy boost before going on to play with your mates or do your homework.
- **Communication**: new advertising couldn't have worked to deliver the new vision without the changes to the packaging and distribution, but it played a key role. The new communication was able to activate and energise these mix changes by showing a famous UK athlete called Daley Thompson using the brand as part of his training regime to achieve peak performance. The soundtrack was a rousing and noisy heavy metal track and ended with a series of traffic lights going from red to lucozade (orange/amber) to green for go.

Sales of the 250 ml bottle exploded by 40% as a result of the re-launch and there was even an increase of 4% on the original large bottle. The re-launch also succeeded in changing

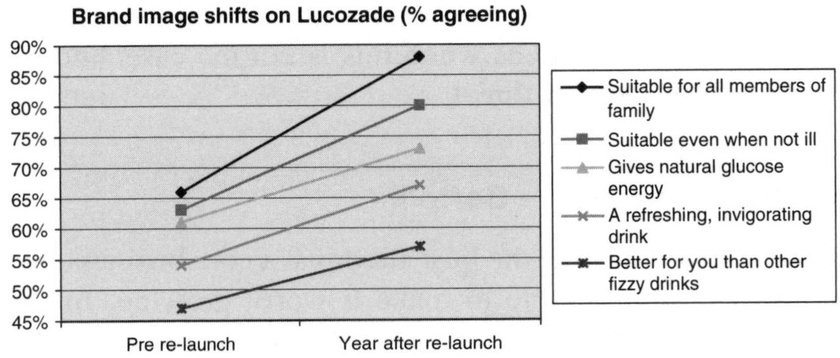

Brand image shifts on Lucozade (% agreeing)

Figure 5.3: Lucozade re-visioning impact.
(Source: Smith, G. (1992) *Lucozade: A Case History,* IPA Advertising Effectiveness Paper).

perceptions of the brand in line with the new vision (see Figure 5.3).

Step 3: a true sports drink

With the core business in growth and the brand re-positioned as a younger and more vibrant energy drink, the foundation was in place for further innovation. A new extension called Lucozade Sport was launched that created the UK sports drinks market. Lucozade Sport is a more technically advanced product that has scientific research to back up the claims it makes about helping sports people recover faster from physical activity. As with the original re-launch, the brand has gone beyond communication to deliver the vision with distinctive packaging and excellent use of celebrity endorsement from sports stars such as Formula 1 drivers Jenson Button and Lewis Hamilton. Despite major investment from global brands Powerade (owned by Coca-Cola) and Gatorade (owned by Pepsico), Lucozade has maintained a strong leadership position in the UK sports drinks market, with a 62% market share.

An important thing to note in the Lucozade story is that the core product remained unchanged, as it was still fundamentally relevant. We will conclude this chapter by looking at what happens when this is not the case, and the core product is under threat.

Re-define the core – Bertolli

In some cases, despite the best attempts, a core business may be just too unprofitable to make it worth growing. In this case there may be an opportunity to re-define the core business, drawing on the positive equity in the brand. The Bertolli brand was famous in the USA for olive oil and had a leading position. However, the business was low margin and subject to fluctuation in the cost of goods relating to olive harvests. Unilever was able to leverage all the positive associations of olive oil (natural, vital, Italian, authentic) and create a new core business in frozen dinners for two. This product used patented technology to create a much better-tasting product than the incumbent Leader Brand in frozen meals. Bertolli positioned the product at a premium price, as an alternative to eating out. This has become a huge and profitable business. The final act of transforming the core came with Unilever's decision to sell the olive oil business.

Another interesting way the core can be re-defined is if a new part of the business grows so well that the 'centre of gravity' of the brand shifts. An example of this might be the Apple brand. The brand originally sold PCs and for many years this remained the core business. New launches failed to make any significant impact on the business, including digital cameras, the Newton digital personal organiser and printers. However, the last 10 years have seen a dramatic transformation of the business, perhaps the most dramatic ever seen. Starting with the launch of the iPod in 2001, Apple morphed into what could be described as a personal entertainment and productivity business. The iPod was followed by two more blockbuster product innovations, the iPhone and iPad. These were amplified by not one or two, but three service innovations: the iTunes store, the App store and the Apple retail stores. Looking at the business today, you could argue that the brand's core business has become the iPhone, as defined as the main source of profit and source of authority.

Re-invent the core – Kodak and TomTom

This is the most challenging and risky situation a core business can be in. In this case, the whole category in which the core business operates is threatened by radical, discontinuous change. This is often caused by new technology making the value proposition of the core business unattractive or even redundant. This is a topic worthy of a book in its own right, so we will only be able to touch on it here. We will look first at an example of the fatal effect of a brand failing to re-invent the core: Kodak. Then, we look at a brand that has been more successful at re-inventing the core: TomTom.

Marketing inertia – Kodak

Kodak is a recent and dramatic example of the need for re-invention and what happens when you fail to act fast enough. Unfortunately Kodak is not alone in paying the price for not re-inventing the core. Examples of other brands which failed to re-invent their core include Blockbuster video rental and, in the UK, Clinton's Cards.

Kodak filed for bankruptcy as this book was being written. The company had gone from having 145 300 employees in 1988 to only 19 900 in 2009. Kodak was, of course, the leading brand in the film-roll market. However, the brand failed to move fast enough to adjust to the growth in digital photography.

Interestingly, Kodak's problem wasn't lack of technology. The company actually invented the first digital camera in 1975, but Kodak's first digital camera was not launched until 13 years later, in 1988. The focus stayed firmly on the core film business, even though by the early noughties one article suggested 'Not a day went by (at Kodak) when there wasn't a discussion about when film would be replaced by digital' (2).

So, Kodak's slowness in changing its core business by driving digital harder and faster didn't reflect 'marketing myopia', which is not seeing the change coming. Rather, the issue for Kodak and other leading brands which have seen their core business eroded was 'marketing *inertia*': being stuck in the old ways of running your core, even though you know change is happening. There are several reasons this can happen:

- Slow technology take-up: the growth of new technology can be gradual at first, before really taking off.
- False security: partly reflecting the slow technology take-up, the core business may continue to grow for some time. In Kodak's case the core film business was still growing at the end of the 90s, up 6.5% in 1999.
- Cost of change: new technology requires investing heavily in new competences and capital, whilst millions of dollars and years of blood, sweat and tears have been invested in the existing business.
- Disrespect of upstart competition: senior management is sometimes disrespectful of smaller, start-up companies, failing to see the long-term threat they may pose.

In cases like Kodak, refreshing the core business is futile, it's like 're-arranging the deckchairs on the Titanic'. Leader brands with a terminally ill core need to re-invent the core by delivering the same benefit in a radically new way.

As the established brand leader, Kodak had great equity to leverage to become the leader of the future. However, re-inventing the core is incredibly difficult, as it requires an acceptance that the established core is going to die. Management needs to go through a proper mourning process of anger, denial and acceptance. There may also be a need to overcome arrogance about new start-ups and treat them with the respect they deserve.

There are several ways to go about re-inventing the core:

- Re-invent from within: create the new competences and technology yourself. This is what Tesco did with online retailing, creating its own system for doing this.
- Create a 'spin-off' business: give new management the freedom to operate in a different way and even have a different culture.
- 'Place bets' on new start-ups: make investments in young start-ups that are attacking your core business. The cost of these investments could be small compared to the loss in future revenue.

Kodak did make some belated attempts to re-invent its core. For example, the Kodak Gallery online photo-storage system has 75 million users. It is an example of the company using option three above, by buying a stake in and then later buying 100% of a start-up, in this case, Ofoto. However, this was too little, too late.

Re-invention – TomTom

TomTom is a fascinating example of a business trying to re-invent its core. TomTom grew rapidly from 2004 onwards following the launch of satnav devices for cars that help you navigate to your destination. However, many smartphones now have built-in satellite navigation and maps at no extra cost for users. This has led to TomTom's core market undergoing disruptive change. The announcement of a deal to provide mapping software for iPhones suggests that it may yet succeed, unlike Kodak which failed to re-invent its core.

Renovate before you need to

Core renovation means proactively upgrading and improving the core when the business is doing well. However, as we saw with Kodak, companies are often too slow to renovate their core. This can be fatal when there is the threat of disruptive change. Part of the problem is the storm of change may take a while to show its full force and, for a while, the company's sales will tick along nicely. This can be seen with TomTom, which, as recently as 2010, had revenues that were still rising, up 3% versus the year before. The storm then hit. Smartphone sales exploded and TomTom's business imploded:

- Revenue down from €1.67 billion in 2008 to €1.27 billion in 2011, a drop of 24%.
- Share price down from €60 in October 2007 to €3 now.
- Market in latest year down one third in North America (2.1 to 1.4 million units) and down 20% in Europe (2.4 to 2 million units).

Re-define your market

A crucial step in re-inventing the core is to re-define the market, based on consumer benefits not products. In the case of TomTom, this means re-defining the market as 'personal navigational services' rather than 'satnavs'. This helps identify threats and opportunities beyond the current products, such as smartphones. This new definition of the core helps inspire and guide re-invention of the core. For TomTom this means repositioning from being a seller of satnavs to selling software and services. As CEO Harold Goddijn comments (3): 'It's our ambition to enable customers to use world-class applications. Whether it's on a smartphone, in a dashboard or on a website, that doesn't really matter'.

Keep the cannibals in the family

TomTom has quickly realised that you're better off having the cannibals inside the family. In other words, if the market is moving from satnavs to smartphone software, you may as well get more than your fair share of the new business, and here TomTom is working on several fronts to re-invent the core:

- Smartphone software: the recent announcement of a partnership with Apple for the iPhone drove TomTom's share price up 20% by itself. TomTom has also signed a deal with Research In Motion Ltd to provide maps and real-time traffic information on its BlackBerry smartphones.
- In-car navigation: providing special software for Internet-enabled phones following the purchase of TeleAtlas in 2008 to get the necessary software, technology and content to connect cars with the Internet.
- Insurance companies: providing technology for UK insurance broker Motaquote's Fair Pay Insurance product. This bases premiums on driving behaviour, rewarding good driving with lower premiums.

The need for speed

The challenge with re-inventing the core is to move fast enough. TomTom's founder Harold Goddijn says 'Deep at heart we are a software company. That has never changed'. He calls satnavs 'an expensive packaging for software'. However, the transition from selling satnavs to software is not happening fast enough to protect TomTom's total sales (4), as Figure 5.4 shows. Software sales are going up, but hardware sales are going down even faster.

Keep it real

I believe one reason that companies like Kodak, Blockbuster and Clinton's Cards are failing to re-invent their core business is because they are not close enough to the market and the customer. The risk is to be too inwardly focused, worrying about your own business model and asset base. So, it's good to see that Harold Goddijn is trying to 'keep it real' and have an outward focus, saying in the FT article: 'I'm trying to stay in touch as much as I can with the basics. When I'm travelling abroad, I test all my applications for local conditions to see how we have adapted to them'. He also likes to work in the TomTom shop near his Amsterdam headquarters.

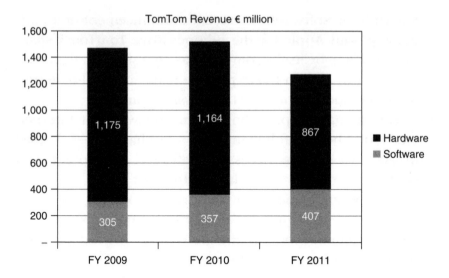

Figure 5.4: TomTom trying to re-invent the core.
(Source: TomTom Annual Reports).

In conclusion, TomTom shows the need to re-invent your core when the market you operate in is undergoing disruptive change. The challenge is to re-define your core market based on benefits, as a start-point for core renovation, and then to execute this at speed, so sales of the new core offering can off-set the decline in the old business model.

 Key takeouts

1. The first step in growing the core is to assess the health of the core brand and business, and the market in which the core brand operates.
2. For a relatively healthy core brand, the best approach is ongoing waves of renovation activity, with each one arriving before the core can start to decline.
3. If the core brand and business is less healthy or even sick, more radical change may be needed to re-position or re-invent the brand.

Checklist 5. Renovation or re-invention?

	Yes	No
• Have you thoroughly assessed the health of your core brand business?	☐	☐
• Have you also looked at the health of the market in which the core brand operates, including the potential threat from disruptive innovation?	☐	☐
• Have you used the results of your health check to agree the core brand growth strategy: renovation, re-position or re-invention?	☐	☐

 ## Handover

You have now seen how to assess the health of your core brand and business and determine the right growth strategy. I will now focus on the most common strategy, core brand renovation, and look at the need to remember and refresh what made your brand and business famous in the first place.

GROW THE CORE WORKOUTS

PART III

Workout 1: Bake the brand into your product

CHAPTER 6

Headlines

The best place to start growing the core is with the core product or service. The challenge here is 'baking in' to the product the brand's distinctiveness. This could be done by uncovering and amplifying a brand truth that the brand already has. However, it may be necessary to upgrade the core, which can be done by giving the consumer more of what they want, taking existing benefits to new levels. Or, it may involve giving consumers less of what they don't want, removing or reducing negatives that could be barriers to trial and so restrict the core brand's penetration.

Some of the most inspiring examples of core brand growth I've seen and blogged about in recent years come from brands which have a zero advertising budget; brands such as The Geek Squad, Lush cosmetics and innocent smoothies. And these are not small brands. Several of them have grown their core business to more than £100 million in sales. But how is it possible to create a distinctive brand and drive penetration without any communication budget?

Bake in your brand – The Geek Squad

The key to using product to make your brand distinctive can be found in the words of Founder and 'Chief Inspector' of PC repair firm The Geek Squad, Robert Stephens: 'Advertising is a tax for having an unremarkable product'. His provocative point of view is that if you make every bit of your brand experience distinctive, then you have less need for conventional advertising. In effect, the brand is 'baked in' to the product or service, to borrow from the book with this title by Alex Boguski and John Winsor (1). In effect, the product

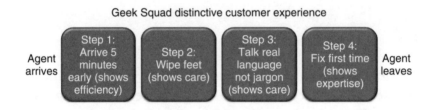

Geek Squad distinctive customer experience

Figure 6.1: Baking distinctiveness into the product.

is the advertising. This approach helped Stephens grow The Geek Squad from nothing in 1994 to now employing 15 000 'agents' with limited advertising. He did this by looking at the entire end-to-end experience of PC repairs and then trying to make each part of the consumer journey distinctive (2). At each step there is a 'proof-point' that makes the service better and communicates the brand (Figure 6.1):

- **Geekmobiles**: rather than turning up in anonymous white vans, The Geek Squad turned up in highly distinctive cars. The first vehicle was a vintage 1958 Simca. As the company got bigger and needed more cars, it went for VW Beetles but designed in black and white colours to mimic police cars.
- **Arrive on time**: Geek Squad agents are trained not just to arrive on time, but 5 minutes early.
- **Wipe your feet**: This sounds basic, and it is. But when was the last time a repairman acted like that?
- **Standout staff**: Instead of 'technicians' or 'service representatives' The Geek Squad has 'agents' dressed like 1960s TV-show police cops. Their uniform includes a white short-sleeve shirt, black shoes, clip-on tie (to avoid being strangled by the tie getting caught in a printer!) and, of course, an official Geek Squad badge. You notice, remember and maybe talk about these guys when they come to help you out.
- **Talk real language**: Geek Squad agents are trained to talk not in computer jargon ('Your RAM needs increasing from

1 Gb to 2 Gb') but rather in real language ('Your computer's brain is full … it needs some more memory space').

- **Problem sorted**: most importantly of all, Geek Squad agents are really good at what they do. After all, they are geeks who know a lot about computers. In consumer surveys they come out top in customer satisfaction versus other repair firms.

Every bit of the product or service can be made more distinctive. Stephens talks, for example, about writing mundane and forgotten bits of brand experience such as warranties in an 'on-brand way'. Have a look below how the company asks for new hires on the job section of its website:

> Recruits wanted to eliminate all evil computer behaviour. Faint of heart need not apply. Geek Squad candidates undergo a gruelling screening process—not unlike that of the FBI. If you've got drive, strong customer relations skills, and a mildly odd affinity for government-chic attire, you may be Geek Squad material.

But my favourite story about baking in the brand is related to something even more mundane: the agents' shoes. With 15 000 agents, Stephens was offered Geek Squad branded shoes with a nice logo on the side. Instead, he asked for the logo to be reversed out *on the sole of the shoe*. Why? Because this meant that everywhere they walked, Geek Squad agents left branded footprints! Think about it for a second, 15 000 agents equals 30 000 shoes. With just one set of footprints a day, that's 150 000 free GRPs (*Gross Rating Points* or actual advertising impressions) a working week, or 75 million a year!

A good creative exercise to stimulate your creativity on your own brand is to try to 'do a Geek Squad'. Imagine your advertising budget is cut to zero and you are an entrepreneur running the business. How would you make your product or service more interesting by baking the brand into every bit of it?

Having introduced the principle of using your product as a way of growing the core, we will now look at several different ways of doing this:

- Amplifying a brand truth: amplifying a distinctive feature of your core product.
- More of what you want: upgrading the core to deliver more of the benefits consumers are interested in.
- Less of what you don't want: upgrading the core to remove barriers to using the brand, and so increasing penetration.

Using product to grow your core 1: Amplify a product truth – Morrisons and Castle Lite

The first way of using the core product to create distinctiveness and so drive penetration is finding and amplifying a brand truth you already have. We'll look at a couple of examples of this approach, one on a service brand and another on a product brand.

Morrisons: distinctive customer experience

The UK supermarket chain, Morrisons, is a good example of this. Here is a business clearly focused on the core, as CEO Dalton Philips said: 'We will be better in food because we focus on food. It's 90% of our in-store business. It's our core and we will make it stay that way'.

As discussed earlier, the distinctiveness, in this case making and preparing more fresh food in store than anyone else, is baked into the product. This approach has helped Morrisons deliver good business results in today's tough times: turnover in 2011 was up 7% and profit up 8%. Here's how they've done it.

Building on a brand truth
Morrisons was re-launched in 2007 to turn around a declining market share. The re-launch aimed to challenge consumer

perceptions about the brand being good on value for money and promotions but not on food quality. What is so smart about the re-launch is the way it was built on product truths embedded in Morrisons' business model. This is focused on preparing and selling fresh food in store, which, in turn, is seen by consumers as being better quality:

- Strategic supply chain: Rather than buying all its food from suppliers, Morrisons has three abattoirs, three bakeries and six fruit and vegetable packhouses of its own. This allows it to ensure freshness, control quality and reduce costs.
- Local produce: 100% British fresh beef, pork, lamb and poultry, 100% sustainable fresh fish, 100% own-brand British free-range eggs.
- Skilled in-store staff: more craft-skilled staff preparing more fresh food in store than any other supermarket – over 6,000 people.

Distinctive customer experience

The genius of Morrisons is to have brought to life the brand truth of freshness in the customer experience with a distinctive in-store property called 'Market Street' (Figure 6.2). This

Figure 6.2: Brand property to make the product distinctive. Reproduced by permission of Wm Morrison Supermarkets Plc.

is a part of the store where you can find a collection of fresh-food stalls, such as a bakers, fishmongers and butchers and these are not just for show. As discussed earlier, these stalls are staffed by well-trained and skilled employees.

Market Street is a powerful and distinctive brand property which really helps Morrisons communicate freshness and stand out from the competition. It cleverly taps into the desire of consumers to have the convenience of a supermarket AND the personal touch of a local food seller.

Brand storytelling

The brand communication did a great job of telling the freshness story in an entertaining and memorable way. The ads showcased features such as freshly prepared fish and meat, that you could try out for yourself in store. Consistency over five years should have helped to build memory structure, with the same music, 'Shine' by Take That, and use of Market Street as a key property and this was all summed up with a strong and simple tagline: 'Fresh for you today'.

Focus on fresh food

What's also interesting is the company's different business model for selling non-food goods (TVs, fridges, clothes, CDs etc.). These have been an important part of the sales mix for big hypermarkets like Tesco, but Morrisons plan to serve these via the online channel. This may prove to be very smart given the way that many of these 'durable' goods are increasingly bought online. Philips describes his approach as follows: 'Hypermarkets will be a blip in retail history. For thousands of years, people have shopped in vibrant markets, not soulless sheds'.

Castle Lite: distinctive product

Leveraging distinctiveness in your product works on simpler brands not just service brands. A good example of this is the Castle Lite brand in South Africa, which has employed this approach to drive several years of double-digit volume growth. The Castle Lite story brilliantly illustrates the idea of distinctiveness being more important than differentiation that we saw earlier in the book. One of the key benefits of beer is refreshment. If, like me, you're a beer fan, nothing hits the spot like a nice cold beer. But surely this is a generic benefit and so not an interesting territory to play in? In fact, it's a great place to play, if you can do what the Castle Lite team did and come up with a distinctive way of bringing this benefit to life. The brand's idea was to sell not just any type of refreshment, but rather 'ice cold' refreshment. Now, even this idea could provoke a response of 'Ice cold. Any brand could do that!' And, in theory, any brand could. However, Castle Lite executed brilliantly and at speed to create the memory structure linked to this idea, effectively taking this position and making it hard for another brand to do the same. The key to the success of Castle Lite is the way the ice-cold refreshment product idea has been amplified across the whole marketing mix (Figure 6.3).

Figure 6.3: Amplifying a distinctive product story. Reproduced by permission of SAB Miller plc.

Packaging

The ice-cold refreshment idea was also brought to life on the bottle, with a 'snow castle' device. This additional brand property was used to indicate when the beer was ice cold, turning blue when the bottle is cooled to $-4\,^{\circ}\mathrm{C}$. This is a clever way of using the brand's castle symbol to help communicate the benefit, rather than creating a whole new visual device.

In-trade

To deliver the ice-cold refreshment benefit, Castle Lite leveraged the incredible distribution system that brand owner SAB Miller has in South Africa. Hundreds of sales people still visit individual taverns and pubs and work on in-trade display and product presentation. This allowed Castle Lite to introduce Ice Cold Fridges into outlets. This ensured the product was served ice cold to deliver maximum refreshment. It has an additional and very important benefit of dramatically improving the in-trade visibility of the brand.

Communication

A clever bit of creative magic is the next part of the Castle Lite success story. TV advertising was used to amplify the ice-cold refreshment idea. Importantly, this communication brought to life the ice-cold fridge as a distinctive visual property. It featured a poor bar man struggling to hold the Castle Lite beer as it was ice cold, throwing it backwards and forwards from hand to hand. The ad used a retro music track, 'Can't touch this', from MC Hammer, who even appeared at the end of the ad. The beauty of this commercial, which you can watch on the brandgym blog, is telling a simple product story in a highly entertaining and memorable way.

Activation

Finally, the brand's activation is aligned to bring to life and amplify the ice-cold refreshment. For the off-trade outlets, such as bottle shops, it uses promotions which are appealing to both customers and consumers alike and further brings to life the product truth, such as patio coolers (this is South Africa remember!), mini-fridges and ice boxes. The brand also ran a contest where people won a trip to, you guessed it, the world's biggest ice bar in Iceland.

Using product to grow your core 2: More of what you want – McDonald's

Upgrading the core is an approach to growing the core that is often overlooked, as the temptation is often to put the innovation efforts behind adding new products to the core range (that we will come back to later), rather than improving the existing products. Upgrading the core can help create 'news', attract new users into the brand and so drive up penetration. Being an ex-Procter & Gamble man, it's a subject close to my heart. The company has a relentless drive to improve the performance of its core products, never accepting that the ceiling has been reached. New products are systematically 'blind-tested' against the current version and competition and need to deliver a statistically significant improvement in order to progress.

The first way to upgrade the core is to offer people more of what they want. The impressive turnaround of McDonald's is a great example of this, with an extensive programme to upgrade the whole customer experience. After a crisis in 2005, when global profits fell dramatically, the company delivered 40 straight months of positive worldwide sales increases. Between 2003 and 2008 the stock price more than tripled, with double-digit increases in earnings per share for the past three years. An interview with UK Marketing Director, Jill McDonald, shed some light on what drove these impressive results (3) on how McDonald's upgraded the core:

1. **Store revolution**: The store design transformation started in 2006 with a move to more vibrant colours, less aggressive

red and contemporary furniture instead of plastic chairs. Free WiFi was also offered. As McDonald commented: 'The new-look restaurants are so visible, and symbolise that something's changed. It's still McDonald's, but it looks different – more modern and fresher'.

2. **Focus on hero products**: CEO Steve Easterbrook led the process of re-building belief in the core burger business and ensured this was delivered with excellence. This involved a massive investment in kitchen equipment to allow improved cooking of food.

3. **Healthy options**: the core business is burgers, but healthy options like fruit bags and carrot sticks have been added. Before you poo-poo these as window dressing, check out the sales data that McDonald quotes: since launching five years ago they have sold 30 million fruit bags. In addition, salt levels in French fries and McNuggets have been reduced.

The approach of offering more of what you want can also work on simpler product brands, not just service brands. A good example of this is Galaxy chocolate, which took its product truth to a whole new level, helping it out-grow its key competitor, Cadbury's Dairy Milk. The brand is positioned as being 'your partner in chocolate indulgence'. The product truth to support this idea is the smoothness of the chocolate, with the brand having a famous advertising endline of 'Why have cotton, when you can have silk?'. Brand owner Mars invested in really amplifying this product truth on several levels:

• Shape: a 'wave' design was introduced to make the little squares of chocolate themselves smoother in shape, in contrast to the sharp edges of Cadbury's Dairy Milk, the leading competitor. This made the in-mouth taste experience much smoother (Figure 6.4).

Figure 6.4: Upgrading the core, with more of what you want. Reproduced by permission of Mars Chocolate UK Ltd.

- Chocolate: the chocolate itself was refined to make it taste smoother.
- Packaging: even the feel of the wrapper itself was improved to make it feel smoother.

Using product to grow your core 3: Less of what you don't want – Walkers

The second way to upgrade the core can be seen in the food and drinks industry over the last few years. Core upgrade focus has moved away from adding new stuff to taking out the bad stuff. In reaction to increasing consumer concerns about the negative effects of artificial colours, flavours and preservatives, companies have invested heavily in taking out these nasty ingredients. Indeed, 'no nasties' is fast becoming a 'table-stake' for food and drink brands: important, but not differentiating. Now even your technicolor Smarties from Nestlé are free from artificial colours and flavours.

The other type of nasty ingredients companies are working on taking out are the ingredients that make us fat. Pepsico's UK brand of potato chips, Walkers, is a good example of a brand that has invested heavily in this area. This is partly to differentiate the brand, but also perhaps a way of trying to pro-actively 'put its house in order' and head off punitive measures from regulatory bodies. Over a period of several years Walkers cut the saturated fat content in its product, with each change a gradual one so that people got used to the taste by degrees. Eventually the change was announced, with a 33% reduction in saturated fat being claimed. This patient approach had the benefit of creating more impact and news value than announcing each small change. Dramatic adverts were able to make the claim that a normal bag of Walkers only had the same saturated fat as half a chocolate biscuit.

 Key takeouts

1. One of the most powerful ways of growing the core is to 'bake' your brand's distinctiveness into the product or service.
2. The first thing to look for is whether you already have a brand truth that can be amplified in a distinctive way.
3. The other main way of harnessing the power of product to grow the core is to upgrade the core, either by offering more of what you want or less of what you don't want.

 Checklist 6. Renovation or re-invention?

	Yes	No
• Have you looked hard at your core product or service to see what is already distinctive?	☐	☐
• Have you considered opportunities to upgrade the product to give people more of what they want?	☐	☐
• Have you looked at barriers to penetration on the core product or service that could be addressed?	☐	☐

Handover

You have now seen the first way to use distinctiveness to grow the core through your product. I will now move on to show you the next way of making your brand more distinctive through harnessing the power of brand identity.

Workout 2: Create a distinctive identity

CHAPTER 7

Headlines

A distinctive and ownable 'brand identity' is essential to stand out in today's over-crowded world, whether this be on supermarket shelves or in the online space. Brand identity plays a key role in creating distinctive brand properties, such as symbols, shapes, colours and type-faces, that can build the memory structure needed to help your brand get chosen at the point of purchase. The most obvious use of identity is in packaging design, but it can also turbo-charge the rest of the marketing mix. As with core brand growth in general, the challenge with identity is to strike the right balance between consistency over time and freshness to keep the brand distinctive and up to date.

Brand identity is at the very heart of creating distinctiveness for the core brand. The most visible role that identity plays is in the design of packaging for the thousands of consumer goods we have to choose from during our shopping trips to the supermarket. But brand identity is much more than just the brand's logo. It's about creating distinctive brand properties that can turbo-charge the whole marketing mix, as we will see later on in the Felix story.

Identity crisis

The role of identity in general, and packaging design in particular, is often misunderstood. In many cases brand identity is expected to help communicate the whole of a brand's positioning. This leads to the creation of what I call 'arrow diagrams', often as a result of over-researching pack designs in focus groups. Each arrow points to a different bit of the pack design and describes what specific benefit or message it is supposed to communicate. I've seen diagrams like this suggesting a single pack design can communicate four or five different messages. This approach is flawed, as it fails to reflect how we respond to packaging in real shopping situations.

As discussed earlier, the only way we can choose 30 items from the 30 000 in a supermarket in 30 minutes is by not thinking. Rather, we shop mainly by acting on auto-pilot, drawing on the hard-wired associations in our brains called 'memory structure'.

Being the 1 in 1000

But if brand identity is not about communicating the brand's positioning and key benefits, then what the hell is it for? The clue is in the name: the role of brand identity is to identify the brand. It really is that simple and it's increasingly important. As we saw earlier in the book, your brand is trying to be one of the 1 in 1000 products that makes it into your supermarket shopping basket each time you buy. Gone is the perfect PowerPoint presentation of your pack, nicely sitting there in splendid isolation. In its place is an over-crowded shelf of products, all desperately vying for your attention. To make things worse, each brand is trying to be seen through a plethora of promotional messaging. The key to cutting through this clutter is to have a simple, impactful and distinctive brand identity that allows consumers to 'lock on' to your brand and buy it.

Brand identity helps us act on auto-pilot in this way through harnessing the power of brand properties that can take many forms including:

- typefaces – such as the Coca-Cola script;
- colours – the blue of the Nivea tin;
- shapes – the keystone of Heinz;
- symbols – Johnnie Walker's walking man.

Figure 7.1: Distinctive brand identity.

These brand properties in themselves may not have much brand meaning when you see them for the first time. For example, the blue 'lozenge' on Hellmann's mayonnaise in itself doesn't communicate anything (Figure 7.1). Rather, symbols like this can be 'loaded' with meaning over time. Once established in memory structure, brand identity works as a key to unlock this brand meaning in an instant. In the case of Hellmann's, the blue lozenge works a key to unlock meaning about being the original and best-tasting 'real' mayonnaise.

Design equities can also cover the structural or '3D' part of a brand, not just the visual side. Indeed, structural packaging is a big opportunity to improve distinctiveness and stand out. Examples include Coke's famous 'contour' bottle, Evian packs that mimic the mountains where the water comes from and the iconic Absolut vodka bottle, star of over 1400 press adverts.

I suggest the way we look at packaging and design in real life is a bit like taking a photo. We look at a piece of packaging and 'snap!' goes our shutter. What we have is an image, a holistic whole, and not a series of arrows pointing to parts of the pack. If the identity is strong and distinctive, this image will serve as the key to unlock the meaning, and encourage us to act and purchase.

Balancing freshness and consistency – Tropicana

As I explained earlier in the book, core brand renovation requires a careful balancing act between consistency on the one hand and freshness on the other. This same approach applies to brand identity. The first step of any identity process should be a careful analysis to understand your brand's visual equities today. Too often brand teams rush into a design process without doing this first step and so risk changing too much.

Design disaster

Tropicana's disastrous design change in the USA is a sobering reminder of the risks with this aspect of growing the core. The change in question, made in January 2009, was not a cheap one. Tropicana paid design guru Peter Arnell a hefty sum for the new look, which he claimed had been 'engineered to imply ergonomically the notion of squeezing'. The new pack lasted only seven weeks before Pepsico pulled it, following complaints from disgruntled Tropicana consumers. One article on the case pointed out that Tropicana's sales in 2009 fell by 20% (1).

The new design ditched two key equities: i) a visual of an orange with a straw stuck in it, used for years and years in pack and communication; ii) the brand logo with a leaf on the 'i'. The logo was shrunk and turned on its side so it was vertical. The result was a breaking of the memory structure built up over many years, and a much more generic pack. As consumers rightly pointed out in complaint letters, the new packaging resembled 'a generic bargain brand' or a 'store brand'. The risk with this decreased branding and loss of visual equities was that people wouldn't find the brand easily enough and so would buy another brand or own label, and if they liked what they bought, especially at a lower price, they might never come back.

Visual equities audit

Carrying out a visual equities audit can help avoid design disasters like Tropicana's. This helps you select the visual equities that are strong and distinctive enough to be part of the memory structure that helps people choose your brand. One simple but effective way of helping identify visual equities is to ask consumers to draw the brand's design using coloured pencils. This can help uncover which visual equities have been stored as memory structure and which are more secondary. This is more effective than showing consumers your current design and asking 'What do you think about this design?', a question that forces people to think rationally. A more sophisticated approach can be to use quantitative research to expose consumers to different visual equities for a very short time. This means they don't have time to think rationally, being forced to react on auto-pilot, a bit like they would in a typical purchase situation.

A similar framework to the one introduced earlier on brand positioning can help summarise the findings from the visual equities audit:

- Keep: critical visual equities that are part of the memory structure used to help identify and choose your brand.
- Lose: visual devices which are adding clutter and complexity and not helping make your brand distinctive.

- Add: elements which are missing from your brand identity and are needed to make it more distinctive.

Using the visual equities audit as a start-point, the challenge is then to select and amplify the one or two visual devices that are key to helping your brand be distinctive, cutting out the other clutter. Andy Knowles of design agency JKR calls this process of selecting and amplifying your visual essence creating 'brand charisma'. The advantage of this approach is that your brand's visual essence is hard for own-label brands to copy. In contrast, falling into the trap of filling your whole pack with nice shots of the product makes your design much easier to copy.

The visual equities audit can help guide you in the delicate act of balancing consistency and change from an identity standpoint.

The brand identity challenge will vary depending on the strength of the current identity and the context your brand is in. Here, you will discover five different approaches:

- Updating your identity: for a brand with a strong, distinctive identity where the emphasis is on consistency;
- Creating an identity: for a brand lacking visual equities, where the focus is on freshness;
- Re-positioning: going a step further to use brand identity to re-position the brand altogether;
- Adding value: using brand identity to add value to the brand experience;
- Packvertising: using the whole of the pack to communicate.

Updating your identity – Nivea

At one extreme of the spectrum between freshness and consistency is the handful of brands in the enviable position of having a strong and even iconic brand identity. In this case the challenge is to keep as much consistency as possible to build on the strong memory structure. A great example of

Figure 7.2: 50 years of fresh consistency.

this is Nivea's core product, Nivea Creme (Figure 7.2). The product was launched in 1911, and from 1925 it was sold in the highly distinctive round blue tin. What is most impressive is that the key visual equities we see today have been used pretty consistently for over 50 years since 1959:

- Blue colour;
- Nivea name in upper case;
- Creme written in same typeface;
- Same round tin;
- Pure, clean and uncluttered design.

Creating your identity – Charlie Bigham's

At the other extreme of the fresh consistency spectrum are brands that are lacking a strong identity; a visual equities audit would show up very little to build on. In this case, the challenge is to create a distinctive identity, building on some form of truth about the brand. This brand truth could be to do with the name of the product, where it comes from, a key benefit or how it's made.

Charlie Bigham's is an example of a brand creating an identity. This small, but fast growing, UK food company is named after the founder, who still runs the company and leads recipe creation. Bigham's make lovely meals which are ready to cook, such as moussaka, lasagne and pies. The food is nicely presented, with pies, for example, coming in enamel ramekins you can re-use. It looks the real thing and it tastes great; it really does deliver a nice dinner for two for a fraction of the price of eating out.

When Tom Allchurch joined as CEO, the brand's identity was nice but not very distinctive. Initial positioning work identified the benefit of giving busy couples an opportunity to spend some 'us' time once the kids had finally been packed off to bed. The couple want something better than a bog-standard ready meal but don't have the time or energy to cook from scratch. The brand's role is well summed up by Charlie himself on the packaging, as follows:

> I came up with this brand-new range specially designed to give couples the chance to steal back some time together. So, turn off the phones, dim the lights, crack open a bottle and enjoy a wonderful night in over some really lovely food.

New packaging created with agency Big Fish used a cartoon couple, called The Twosomes, to be much more distinctive (Figure 7.3). Each pack has a different humorous

Figure 7.3: Creating a distinctive identity. Reproduced by permission of Bigham's Ltd.

Figure 7.4: Identity for shelf stand-out. Reproduced by permission of Bigham's Ltd.

cartoon and these help the brand to really stand out on the shelf amongst the 'wall of black' of other premium ready meals (Figure 7.4). Lift the cartoon up and there is an appetising picture of the dish and some words from Charlie. These packs create real stand-out and distinctiveness at the overcrowded supermarket shelf. Tests showed that off-take was significantly improved and this has been backed up by in-market performance. Eighteen months after the re-launch, revenue is up 170%. The Twosomes also have the potential to be a really powerful brand property that can be used in different media, especially online.

Suggesting a benefit – Waitrose Essentials

Beyond just helping the brand stand out, brand identity can help better cue the benefit of a brand. As discussed earlier, this is not about spelling out the benefits in detail, but rather using brand properties as a key to opening the door to the brand's meaning. A good example of this is the re-launch of Waitrose's own-label range (2). This UK retailer has a niche position in the market, focusing on top quality food associated with higher prices. This reputation helped the brand grow nicely for many years, but became a potential hindrance as recession hit in 2008. Indeed, by the end of the year the brand was starting to suffer from a drop in penetration, as shoppers were 'leaking out of the bucket' faster than new ones were being added in. Consumers saw the brand as being a full 25% more expensive than the competition, even though the own-label offer was actually the same price on many everyday own-label items. Part of the problem was that the own-label range had a fragmented brand identity, with a confusing collection of different looking sub-ranges.

The solution was to create a new identity to unify 1200 of Waitrose's everyday staple items, such as bread, cheese and milk (Figure 7.5). This range was cleverly named 'Waitrose Essentials'. By avoiding terms like 'Basic' or 'Value', this avoided tarnishing the brand's quality credentials. The range was launched using communication with the idea 'Quality you'd expect at prices you wouldn't'. The new identity helped increase sales of the lines re-launched by +7.5%, worth £34

Figure 7.5: Identity to cue a benefit.

million a year in revenue and c. £11 million in profit, double
the cost of the re-launch.

Re-positioning – Green & Black's

A step further than amplifying the benefit of your brand
is to use brand identity to re-position it altogether. The
re-design of Green & Black's helped transform it from a
niche, ethical chocolate to a premium indulgence brand.
The brand's organic credentials and bittersweet taste from
its high 70% cocoa content earned it instant niche appeal,
but market share stuck at only 1%. It was sold mainly in
specialist stores and when it was in supermarkets, it was
stuck in the organic section. At the end of the 1990s new
pack designs helped to re-position the brand from worthy
organic to luxury premium chocolate, leading on indulgence
and with organic credentials becoming a reason-to-believe.
Sales rose from £4.5 million to £50 million and the brand
was bought by Cadbury's in 2006.

Adding value – Molton Brown

Brand identity has the power to actually add value to the
usage experience, as shown by the story of Molton Brown's
gift sets. This brand of high-quality toiletries is distributed
in upmarket hotels and posh shops such as Harrods and
Saks. The Christmas gift sets used to be ordinary standard
collections of different products (shampoo, shower gel etc.),
sold in boring boxes or see-through bags. However, Molton
Brown found out through talking both to the end-user
(mainly women) and the buyer (mainly men) that these
Christmas packs were a bit of a second-class gift. A 'distress'
purchase when short of ideas. The brand was good, as were
the individual products, but the presentation let them down.
The other key insight was that most men are *really* lazy
when buying gifts.

Building on these insights, the team transformed the special gift packs by designing a beautiful range of boxes that any man would be proud to offer. But wait, here's the real flash of brilliance. Not only did the buyer of this new pack not need to box up the individual products, but by Molton Brown removing the external branding and adding a fancy ribbon, he didn't even need to wrap it up. Genius!

The business benefits of this move were huge. First, they sold several times more. Second, they were able to charge a much higher premium price. Third, stores loved the packs and so built huge displays of them, boosting both brand visibility and sales.

Packvertising – innocent

As discussed, the main role of brand identity is not to communicate a brand's positioning. Rather, the key role is to make a brand distinctive and so more likely to be chosen at the point of purchase. However, you can use the rest of the pack, beyond the front facing part, as a communication medium, an approach I call 'packvertising'. This approach is most often used by smaller brands that can't afford expensive advertising, with the most famous example being innocent smoothies.

Each bottle or carton of innocent is more like a mini-magazine than a conventional pack. The pack copy has been the main communication channel for getting across the brand's innocent, light-hearted and friendly personality. However, it is important to note the actual consumer-facing front of innocent's packaging is a good example of simple, clean identity, with the focus on the brand name and the innocent 'angel' symbol (Figure 7.6).

What is especially clever, and hard to do, is the way the pack copy changes every few months, creating consumer interest and involvement. Here are some examples:

Figure 7.6: The masters of packvertising.

- Caps that say 'Enjoy by', rather than 'Use by';
- Ingredient lists that say things like '25 blueberries, 10 raspberries and two fat nuns';
- Tips on how to get fit and stay lazy (e.g. knee-bends when sat on the toilet);
- Hidden in the fold of a carton top, 'Email us at iamnosey.innocent.co.uk';
- Product claim 'We use no artificial colours, flavours, or preservatives. And if we do you can tell our mums';
- Separation may occur (but mummy still loves daddy).

Many brands have tried and failed to copy the innocent approach. Talking to the brand's creative genius, Dan Germain, I got some insights on why this is the case. Dan has an in-house creative team of about 15 people working on the brand. These people live and breathe the brand better than any external agency ever could, putting a huge amount of resource behind the packaging, writing on average one new set of pack copy a day! Therefore, before trying to 'do an innocent' with your packaging, check that you have the right creative resource in place to do this not only once, but consistently over many months and years.

Family ties – Nescafé and Red Bull

You have seen how brand identity over time requires a balance between freshness and consistency. Another balancing act is needed over the range as the brand extends the core to offer new versions (a topic we will revisit later). The fancy name for this brand identity task is 'range architecture'. Here, the balancing act has to manage two conflicting objectives:

- Navigation: clearly position the new products so they are easy to find;
- Masterbrand identity: respecting the core brand identity to draw on and reinforce memory structure, so the new addition looks like part of the family.

It's important in range architecture to remember that, as with identity in general, it needs to work intuitively and immediately so people can choose and buy on auto-pilot. I've seen many brand teams spending endless hours debating what names to give different products in a range, and what detailed text to write on the pack. However, this sort of text is rarely recalled and used as it requires too much effort. Talk to real consumers about which product in your core range they buy and they are more likely to say 'the blue one' than 'Extra Moisturising for Dry and Damaged Hair'. This is not to say that naming of products should be overlooked, as the first time the product is bought someone may need to look in detail at the pack. Rather, to help people navigate and find what they want, other brand identity elements are more important.

Good = £4.44   Better = £5.79   Best = £6.67
(index 100)   (index 130)   (index 150)

Figure 7.7: Using identity for intuitive range navigation.

An example of the Nescafé coffee range (Figure 7.7) helps illustrate how range navigation works in reality. Consistency comes from the same Nescafé logo in white, in the same place on each pack. The key elements used to help navigation are:

• Structural packaging: completely different for basic, Gold Blend and Exotic versions;
• Pack colour: black used for the Exotic range, cuing premiumness;
• Pricing: 30–50% price difference;
• Pack graphics: Everyday vs. Special vs. Exclusive;
• And last, range names: Original vs. Gold Blend vs. Alta Rica.

The challenge of getting the right range architecture is shown by the launch of a new core range extension by energy drink Red Bull, called Editions. The range has three new flavours: Silver (lime), Blue (blueberry) and Red (cranberry). I assume the idea of Editions is to address a barrier to trial by changing the taste of the product, as the advertising for

Editions states: 'New tastes, same energy'. Editions' branding fails to build on one of the world's strongest identities. The Red Bull visual identity is very powerful and helps you find Red Bull on auto-pilot. It has several key elements, only very small parts of which are used in Editions:

RED BULL	vs.	EDITIONS
1. The 4-quadrant design	vs.	Block of colour
2. Red, silver, blue	vs.	Red or silver or blue
3. The two clashing bulls in the middle	vs.	Bit of one bull
4. Red Bull name in red, centrally positioned	vs.	Red Bull small, vertical

By breaking all these codes, it looks on the shelf like there are three new products called Blue, Silver and Red and this runs the risk of the new products missing out on trial that would have come from them being more clearly seen as extensions of the strong Red Bull brand. A better balance was achieved with the sugar-free version (Figure 7.8). This kept three of the four key elements of the brand identity (quadrants, name and bull), changing only the colours. This

Figure 7.8: Family ties through brand identity.

means you can distinguish the two versions on shelf, but the sugar-free one still looks like Red Bull.

Amplifying brand properties – Felix

So far I've focused on the creation of distinctive brand properties using brand identity, and the key role they play from a packaging-design standpoint. However, brand identity can play a much bigger role in turbo-charging the core brand mix as a whole. A tale of two cats helps illustrate this.

On the one hand, we have Whiskas, Mars's global catfood brand. Back in 2002, Whiskas had a dominant 30% share of the UK catfood market. On the other hand, we have Felix, lagging behind with only 6% market share. In just five years Felix has boosted its share from 6% to 26%, taking leadership from Whiskas, whose share dropped from 30% to 24%.

The challenge for Felix was that it had roughly one third of the advertising budget of Whiskas. With this limited budget, the only way for Felix to grow was to 'punch above its weight' and get more bang for its branding buck. This required a marketing mix that was more distinctive and memorable, and so better able to create memory structure.

The key brand property Felix harnessed was Felix the cartoon cat from the packaging (Figure 7.9). The brand identity was amplified to do much more than just be the brand's logo. Felix was brought to life using animated, black and white TV commercials. He was portrayed as a loveable rascal that cat owners identified with, in contrast to the perfect, soft-focus cats of the Whiskas' world. In this way, the brand property featured on the pack design was 'loaded' with meaning, as discussed earlier. The brand team didn't just rely on TV to amplify the Felix brand property. They harnessed many other forms of 'free' marketing, including the website, eCards and Felix branded merchandise such as cat bowls and even Felix slippers. According to people who worked on the brand, a screen-saver featuring Felix chasing a ball of wool that was

Figure 7.9: Amplifying a brand property.

seeded with a couple of hundred of people ended up on one million computers!

Interestingly, the brand idea of Felix, 'Cats like Felix like Felix', was pretty close to that of Whiskas' 'Cats would buy Whiskas'. Both brands focused on communicating that the product had a taste cats loved. Felix did not have a differentiated proposition. Rather, Felix had a highly distinctive way of communicating the same, core category benefits. And this meant that every bit of media money invested by Felix got a better return on investment.

Five-minute focus groups

Understanding how identity and design work in the real world has serious implications for how creative work is developed and researched. Most of the focus groups I have seen on packaging design are pretty useless. Guess how they usually start? We ask a bunch of people 'What do you think about this new design?' Straight away, respondents are asked to think in a rational, considered way, accessing the bit of the brain they don't use for most of their shopping. To make things worse, the pack design is often shown in isolation, rather than in a real-life setting on a shelf. Furthermore, to render the results totally and utterly useless, consumers spend 10, 15 or even 20 minutes staring at the designs, when in reality they would spend 30 seconds. At the end of this we end up with consumers starting to act like creative directors, offering views on typefaces, shades of colour and the like.

Here are a few suggestions:

- Always look at the design in context: the first step is to always look at a design in context and not in isolation. Avoid looking at a new design by itself in PowerPoint. Even more artificial is to look at the new pack alongside the current pack, or next to alternative designs, a situation the consumers will never be faced with. Instead, mock up a shelf and place the new pack in a competitive context.
- Ban the 'beauty contests': too often management teams get into debates about whether they like or dislike a new piece of design work. However, this misses the point completely about the role of identity. Design is not there to be liked. The right question to ask is how effective the design is at helping consumers shop quickly, easily and confidently.
- Run five-minute focus groups: stop running extended focus groups that over-expose consumers to packaging and end up with them acting like creative directors. If you do quality research on design, then expose consumers to a piece of new packaging on a mocked-up shelf, see what they pick up and whether the new pack helps them find the brand more easily; then get them to look at the design, exposing them to the pack for no more than 30–40 seconds. Put the pack away and then ask for initial reactions and recall.
- Quantitative findability testing: if doing quantitative testing of new designs, focus this on 'findability'. This involves measuring how quickly consumers can find your new pack on a mocked-up shelf. In this way you can measure 'share of attention' for your design versus your share of

'shelf space'. Advances in online research make this sort of testing a lot easier and more cost-effective than before. Cut out questions about brand image communication and likeability, as these measures are not linked to the true role of brand identity. Especially, get rid of artificial comparisons where consumers are asked to express a preference, between design A and design B for example.

 Key takeouts

1. Distinctive identity plays a central role in growing the core, not only on packaging but also the wider mix.
2. A visual equities analysis will help determine the right balance of freshness and consistency needed in your identity.
3. Brand identity can help the brand stand out in a crowded market, cue the brand benefit and even help re-position the brand.

 Checklist 7. Create your own identity

	Yes	No
• Have you carried out a visual equities analysis to determine the right balance of freshness and consistency needed in your identity?	☐	☐
• Have you worked on ways to amplify the properties from your brand identity to turbo-charge your marketing?	☐	☐
• Have you looked at how your identity works in situ, on the shelf or online, and avoided the trap of reviewing it in isolation?	☐	☐
• If researching your design, are you avoiding the trap of spending too long asking consumers what they think, risking them taking on the role of creative directors?	☐	☐

Handover

You have now seen the role brand identity can play in making your brand distinctive, so it is at the forefront of people's minds when people shop in this category. I will now move beyond the fundamentals of product and identity to show you how to grow the core with distinctive communication.

Workout 3: Communicate with cut-through

CHAPTER 8

Headlines

Many communication campaigns fail to grow the core as they change too often, lack distinctiveness and miss a strong link to the brand. To be more effective, communication needs to deliver fresh consistency. Consistency comes from both a unifying brand story and the creation and amplification of distinctive brand properties that build memory structure. Freshness comes from updating the execution to bring news in the form of chapters of marketing activity. Creating a distinctive communication campaign can be done from scratch or by rejuvenating an old campaign.

Communication breakdown

Communication can play a leading role in creating the distinctiveness needed to drive penetration of your core brand and business. Many of the great examples of renovating or revitalising the core feature strong advertising. Unfortunately, much of the time, effort and money spent on advertising fails to deliver in this way. This reflects some fundamental problems in the way communication is briefed, developed and executed.

Chopping and changing

For most brands, looking at a 15–20 year advertising history is almost like looking at three, four or more different brands. There is a chopping and changing of both the message and the executional properties being deployed. Part of this problem is the 'new broom' syndrome caused by the rapid turnover of marketing directors. New marketing directors will often want to stamp their authority on a brand by changing campaign, often accompanied by an expensive and time-consuming agency pitch. Recruitment experts Spencer Stuart have done research showing that the average tenure of a senior marketer is a mere 22 months. This means that just as the latest campaign is close to creating some memory structure . . . in comes the new person and a likely change in campaign (1).

The problems caused by inconsistent communication can be seen at the mobile network provider, Orange. The brand was the clear leader in the UK, helped by an iconic orange and black visual identity and consistent use of the brand tagline, 'The future's bright. The future's Orange'. The brand had a distinctive style of communication that focused on the human emotions that Orange's mobile network helped create, rather than technical details. This was backed up by a series of service innovations, such as billing by the second not the minute and the introduction of text messaging. However, a take-over by France Telecom led to an exodus of key people, including charismatic and influential founder Hans Snook. There then ensued a raft of different campaigns between 2001 and 2008:

1. Hard-nosed business man.
2. Child as teacher in the Orange mobile school.
3. Animals as metaphors for price plans.
4. Cartoon characters.
5. Human connection when the lights went out in New York.
6. Wind-up toys joined at the waist: Togetherness.
7. Life as you like it.
8. I am.

By 2008 Orange had lost leadership to the O_2 brand, falling to fourth place in both market share and brand imagery. The brand had to spend much more on advertising than O_2 (£90 million vs. £50 million) to support a smaller business, a clear sign of the Orange brand becoming less distinctive.

To be effective, brands need strong leadership to drive consistency over time, avoiding the temptation of novelty for novelty's sake. Rather than changing a campaign every couple of years, the strongest brands are able to refresh a campaign to keep it interesting. Indeed, some of the most effective campaigns have been running not just for several years, but several decades.

Sponsored entertainment

The second problem with communication is when it becomes what I call 'sponsored entertainment', where the team loses sight of the product or service. These expensive Hollywood epics try to get across a higher level philosophy, rather than a specific product message linking it to the brand. The brand is simply a logo that appears at the end of the advert, rather than being the star of the show. The problem with this type of communication is that it risks having limited impact on the bottom line. Divorced of any real brand message, it leaves consumers saying 'So what?' They have a nice warm feeling, but are unlikely to remember your brand.

People may point to brands like Nike, Diesel and Levi's and implore brand teams to create the same sort of emotional communication for their brands. This can work if you are a badge brand where emotional values are key, although the brand still needs to play a starring role and be somehow 'imprinted' on the commercial as a whole, not just the final frame. However, this lifestyle approach is less likely to work if you are selling pasta sauce or pet food, especially true when you are competing with own label products that are 30–50% cheaper than you. A more effective approach is telling a product story in an ownable, impactful way, combining sausage (product) and sizzle (emotion), as the Dove team discovered when communicating its 'beauty theory'.

When the Dove team wanted to celebrate the real beauty of women, free from artificiality and stereotypes, it first developed three different 'brand anthem' campaigns ('Beauty Has A Million Faces, One Of Them Is Yours', 'Give Your Beauty

Wings' and 'Let's Make Peace With Beauty'). Each campaign tried to get women to stop judging themselves so harshly and gave them tips to see that they were already beautiful. However, this approach did not work with women, as the planner from the Ogilvy agency commented (2):

> Unfortunately, women were not impressed. They found our ideas patronising. The tone was a bit happy-clappy. The top-down approach seemed to lead to rather didactic, theoretical and distant work. So we decided instead to work bottom-up – product first, wrapped in beauty theory.

The product the team wrapped in beauty theory was a new firming range of body wash and lotions. These products were applied to hips, bums and thighs to tighten them up. The now famous campaign used real women in their underwear, with all different shapes and sizes of body on show. It was shot without any of the touching up that goes on in most beauty advertising campaigns. The end-line was 'As tested on real curves'. The advertising broke the mould of beauty advertising and so got huge impact, including free publicity valued at an estimated £4.6 million! (3). The business results surpassed expectations, with sales exceeding forecasts by 110% in western Europe. In the UK, sales rose from 280 000 bottles in 2003 to 2.3 million in 2004.

Fresh consistency

Effective advertising creates distinctive memory structure, in contrast to the communication discussed above that chops and changes, or is not linked to the brand. The importance of distinctive memory structure in communication is shown by brain-imaging research done by Thinkbox with researchers at Neuro-Insight (4). In each of nine different categories, a pair of adverts was tested: one advert that was commercially successful and one that was not. The study showed that memory encoding was key to effectiveness:

There is a strong and growing body of evidence to show that what goes into memory correlates with subsequent purchase decisions and behaviour. These memories can be triggered somewhere on the path to purchase and they can impact on our behaviour. What goes into memory is a better predictor of behaviour than articulated recall.

Creating distinctive memory structure with communication requires fresh consistency, a concept introduced earlier in the book. The importance of fresh consistency is backed up by scientific research into the way our brains process information, which was done by Radboud University in the Netherlands and published in a paper by Decode Marketing (5). This shows that too much freshness is ineffective. 'Disruptive' communication that is completely fresh and unexpected grabs attention and gets your brain working. However, this is hard to keep up and needs a high level of involvement and most advertising tends to be processed with low involvement.

On the other hand, too much consistency can be a bad thing. If a signal received by the brain, such as the start of a TV commercial, sets up an expectation which is then confirmed by a subsequent signal, then the reaction of brain cells is reduced. As soon as we expect something and what follows confirms these expectations, our brain switches off and focuses on other stuff.

The optimum approach is to balance freshness and consistency. Many studies have shown that a message that is moderately in line with expectations is the most efficient at increasing attention, liking, recall and recognition. The consistency needed comes from two main sources: the brand story and brand properties.

Consistency – brand story

The first source of consistency is a compelling and relevant brand story that is brought to life in communication in the form of a 'narrative'. The Thinkbox research quoted earlier showed that the first feature of advertising that gets encoded in memory structure is telling a story that triggers an emotional response. Importantly, this story needs to have the brand in a starring role to avoid the problem of sponsored entertainment mentioned earlier, as the authors say: 'What's important for an advertiser is to make sure that their brand is intrinsic to the narrative. Otherwise it's all too easy to get the phenomenon whereby people can remember an advert really clearly, but with no idea at all of what brand is actually being advertised.'

In the case of Carling Black Label, the leading brand of beer in South Africa, the brand story is 'Champion Beer for Champion Men'. This is based on the product truth that the beer has the champion taste, as voted for by expert judges and South African men. The emotional benefit is to inspire, encourage and reward men to be champions in different aspects of their lives.

Consistency – distinctive brand properties

The second form of consistency is the creation and amplification of distinctive brand properties. Here, communication plays a vital role, as it is the way a brand property is 'loaded' with meaning. Over time, if the brand property is used consistently and creates memory structure, it starts to work as a key to unlock brand meaning. So, in the case of Nike's 'swoosh', you now just need to see this logo to immediately unlock brand meaning such as achievement, winning and sports stars. To refer again to the Thinkbox research: 'A key way of boosting the success of a campaign is "iconic triggers" – shapes, colours, sounds or images. If the link between a brand and an "iconic trigger" is constantly repeated and reinforced, the trigger can be used right along the path to purchase.' For example, research by Neuro Insight quoted in the Thinkbox paper showed that the Intel 'chime' sonic branding device boosted memory encoding of the brand by 350%.

Types of brand property

Communication properties can take a multitude of forms. Some of the main ones include:

- Slogans: 'Just Do it' for Nike;
- Celebrity endorsement: John Travolta for Breitling watches;
- Characters: Snap, Crackle and Pop for Kellogg's;
- Colours: red for Coke, blue for Pepsi;
- Pack shape: Absolut vodka;
- Jingles: 'A Mars a day, helps you work, rest and play';
- Sonic device: Intel.

The most powerful brand properties are often used not just over years but over decades. The strongest of these take on cultural meaning, becoming part of everyday language. So, it's not uncommon to hear someone in a business say 'Just Do It!', for example. These sorts of brand properties become true 'brand assets' that add significant value to the brand and make its marketing much more effective.

Sources of brand property

But where do brand properties come from? And how can you go about creating one if you need to? In most cases, a brand property comes from finding a truth about the brand that you can use (Figure 8.1):

- **Name:** the Johnnie Walker brand's global slogan 'Keep Walking' comes from the name of the brand and the walking man symbol which has been on the bottle for many years.
- **Symbol:** the Sure/Rexona brand of deodorant has used the 'tick' symbol on the packaging to dramatise wetness protection in communication over several decades.

Sure/Rexona -   Ben & Jerry's -   Andrex –
Symbol   Founders   Character

Figure 8.1: From brand truth to brand property.

- **Characters:** Andrex toilet tissue has featured the cute puppy from its packaging in its communication for many years.
- **Origin:** Jack Daniels builds all its communication about Lynchburg Tennessee, where the drink is distilled.
- **Founder:** Ben & Jerry's still make use of the brand's founders, long after the brand has been owned by Unilever.
- **Expert users:** the Ray-Ban brand has made use of the fact that the sunglasses were worn by World War II pilots in the US air force.
- **Product truth:** Nurofen's targeted action on pain is brought to life using a target symbol.

In other cases, the brand property is more of a creative leap of inspiration. For example, the Nike slogan 'Just Do It' had a strange source. Dan Wieden of agency Wieden & Kennedy was inspired by the final words of . . . convicted mass murderer Gary Gilmore, who said to the firing squad before his execution: 'Let's do it!'.

Think like a TV producer

To help create a marketing plan that delivers fresh consistency, a good source of inspiration is the world of TV series. Successful TV series, such as *24*, *Friends* and *The Sopranos*, maintain high ratings both within a season of, say, 20 episodes and over multiple 'seasons'. *The Sopranos* managed six seasons and *Friends* an amazing ten. This is achieved through the power of fresh consistency. This is similar to the James Bond story earlier in the book, but even more demanding, as the brand has to remain fresh for 20 episodes per year, not 20 films over four decades.

Each TV show uses fresh consistency. The fundamental story stays the same. For example, *The Sopranos* is the adventures and mishaps of an insecure Mafia mobster who is in therapy. A number of other key creative properties are consistent, such as music, setting and lead characters. At the same time, each episode of the series tells a fresh chapter of the story, with plot twists and character evolutions.

Applying this to your core brand means thinking about your annual marketing plan as a season. The consistency comes from the unifying brand idea and brand properties which help create and amplify memory structure. The freshness comes from a series of integrated 'chapters' of activity on the core brand. Each chapter can use different ways of growing the core, such as activation, packaging or just simple communication.

An example of such a chapter plan is shown in Figure 8.2 for the leading beer brand in South Africa, Carling Black Label. The brand idea of 'Champion Beer for Champion Men' is consistent, as are the key brand properties: red and black colours, the trophy visual device and the bold typeface. Each chapter is then a dramatisation of this brand idea. One chapter is centred on the 'Be a Champion Coach' activation idea, where consumers actually get to pick the

Figure 8.2: Think like a TV series producer. Permission granted by SAB Miller Ltd.

players for one of two leading clubs playing in a local derby. The second chapter focuses on a 'Champion Taste Challenge' to reinforce the brand's superior taste. The final chapter is about being a 'Community Champion' and has a focus on BSR (brand social responsibility).

A key challenge with each chapter is getting the multiple agencies involved to collaborate on how to amplify the activity by getting the whole marketing mix to work together. Instead of building a marketing plan 'horizontally', with rows of activity being part of the mix (advertising, digital, PR etc.) the plan is built 'vertically', by creating the series of integrated chapters of activity.

We will now look at two different ways of creating distinctive communication: i) creating a campaign, ii) remembering and refreshing what made you famous.

Creating a campaign – Sainsbury's

A good example of creating a distinctive communication campaign comes from Sainsbury's, one of the UK's leading retailers (6). Back in 2000 the Sainsbury's supermarket chain was struggling, having lost market leadership to Tesco and with like-for-like sales declining by −0.2%. The brand was seen as having good quality produce but with a personality which was a bit arrogant and elitist. In addition, the brand suffered from advertising which lacked cut-through, with an awareness index (how effective investment is at boosting awareness) roughly half that of key competitor Tesco.

A new CEO, Sir Peter Davies, and Marketing Director, Sarah Weller, set about rejuvenating the brand. The first key decision was to re-focus and celebrate the area that Sainsbury's was famous for, which was quality fresh food. This was summed up with the brand idea 'Making life taste better'. A key objective was to refresh the brand's personality, injecting passion and energy and making it more accessible. The team decided that the best way to bring this idea to life was by using a chef as an advocate for Sainsbury's. In what turned out to be a stroke of genius, the company signed up an up-and-coming young chef called Jamie Oliver. Jamie was passionate about food and cooking, but had a liberated, fun and youthful attitude to food, a real change to the more conventional and rigid approaches to cooking that had dominated books and TV shows. This was summed up with the brand essence from his own positioning tool: 'Get stuck in!' Qualitative research showed that Jamie's personality helped rejuvenate Sainsbury's personality in the way desired, helping create a brand image that was more contemporary, youthful and accessible (7).

Over the next 10 years Sainsbury's ran 100 commercials featuring Jamie Oliver. He was used to showcase 'do-able' recipes with energy and passion, inspiring people to follow his example and make life taste better. For example, the first ad showed Jamie enjoying a drink with friends. As they wander out of their local pub, he invites his companions round for a 'ruby' (rhyming slang for a curry). Stopping off at a late-night Sainsbury's, Oliver picks up the ingredients, knocks up a quick but tasty meal and his friends are wowed by the results.

Jamie was featured in many different chapters of activity, addressing a range of different brand objectives:

• Brand idea: launch of 'Making life taste better'.

- http://www.brandrepublic.com/news/56355/Jamie-Oliver-launches-new-Sainsbury-s-adHealth: Be Good to Yourself range and Active Kids promotion.
- Seasonal: Christmas.
- Premium indulgence: Taste the Difference range.
- Value: Feed your Family for a Fiver promotion.

The power of Jamie as a distinctive brand property is backed up by a host of different data. The brand's advertising had an increased Awareness Index score of 12 vs. the retail average of 6, and was 65% more effective than previous adverts. In the first 21 months alone, the campaign is judged to have delivered £1.12 billion in incremental revenue, according to econometric modelling. By the time Sainsbury's finally parted ways with Jamie Oliver in 2011, the company had enjoyed 23 consecutive, 12-week periods of year-on-year share gains (8).

Refreshing what made you famous – Hovis

On brand vision projects I often witness marketing teams pulling their hair out with frustration as consumer focus groups recall not the latest advertising, but rather commercials from 15, 20 or even 30 years ago. They remember slogans, music and catch-phrases. These are associations that have been 'hard-wired' into our brains to create the memory structure we have been discussing in the book. Once this memory structure is established, it tends to stick. And the harsh truth about those frustrated marketing teams earlier? They have probably failed to create any advertising memorable enough to dislodge the old ads from people's memories and create new memory structure. This was the problem facing Jon Goldstone on the Hovis brand of bread when he arrived as Premier Foods' Marketing Director in early 2008 (9).

In addition to a lack of advertising saliency, the brand had been gradually reducing quality. All this as a key competitor,

Warburtons, was making strong advances. Market share for Hovis fell over 24 months, from 27% in early 2006 to 22% by the end of 2007. This left Hovis trailing 10% behind Warburtons, with whom they had previously shared leadership. If the share trends continued, it was forecast that in a year's time this gap would have increased to 20%. Jon needed to act, and act fast. The share gap with Warburtons was widening and there were rumblings from retailers that the brand was even in danger of being de-listed from some stores, which would have caused sales to spiral down even faster. Rather than try and create a new communication campaign from scratch, Jon took the second route to distinctive communication, which is to remember and refresh what made the brand famous.

Back to those frustrating focus groups from earlier who recall only old advertising. In the case of Hovis, all they remembered was the brand's 'Boy on a bike' commercial from a full 35 years ago. Set to a piece of evocative music, the advert showed a boy in what looks like the 1950s cycling up a hill in order to get a loaf of Hovis bread. Amazingly, this advert was even recalled by people aged 35, who weren't even born when it was aired! This is because the commercial is regularly voted the all-time favourite advert in the UK, receiving loads of free publicity.

With a brief as simple as 'Make Hovis great again', agency MCBD set about remembering and refreshing what made Hovis famous in the Boy on a Bike advert. Certain key elements were used to create consistency, drawing on the memory structure linked to the original ad:

- Boy and his Hovis on a journey.
- Endline: 'As good today as it's always been'.
- The iconic 'little brown loaf', unsliced wholemeal bread.

The freshness came from updating the boy's journey to be one where he runs through the most important events of the last century (e.g. World War II, England winning the

Figure 8.3: PR amplification. Reproduced by permission of Premier Foods plc.

World Cup in 1966, the millennium) and returning safely in 2008 (Figure 8.3). This tapped into a desire for nostalgia and the reliability of tried and trusted brands at a time of uncertainty. In addition, it reminded people of what a great brand Hovis was; one with heritage that had stood the test of time. Freshness also came in bold execution that helped create valuable PR worth an estimated £2 million (Figure 8.4):

- The advert was 122 seconds long, one second for each year of Hovis's history.
- One of the UK's most watched TV shows, *Coronation Street*, cut two seconds from its programme to accommodate the advert.
- Journalists and employees were used as extras in the film.

The benefit of tapping into memory structure to boost distinctiveness was shown in the tracking results, with 86% of people agreeing that 'I would definitely remember the ad was for Hovis'. In two separate polls the ad was also voted campaign of the year by the British public, renewing the

Figure 8.4: Remembering and refreshing what made you famous. Reproduced by permission of Premier Foods plc.

brand's reputation of producing well-recalled and well-loved communication.

In addition to the new communication, a full programme of core renovation was undertaken. This included product improvements to get Hovis back from third to top choice in blind tasting. And a more coherent and impactful packaging design was introduced.

In terms of results, the re-launch increased Hovis's penetration from around 25% to 35%. Share returned to growth, so that by the end of 2008 the gap vs. Warburtons had been cut to 7%. Sales in the year were up 8%, and the brand had re-gained leadership in two key retailers, Asda and Tesco.

What about social media?

Social media* is such a red-hot topic today that I feel the need to give a view on how they can help create distinctive communication to grow the core. Social media are sexy, shiny and new. And scaremongering headlines tell us that the whole world of marketing is changing and that 'old' media like TV are dead.

Well, the first thing to point out as I am writing this book is the lack of robust data on the return-on-investment (ROI) of social media. Who knows, by the time you read it, perhaps there will be more data, given how fast things move. But for now, fads and fashion are the key drivers of use, as shown by a *brandgym* survey with over 100 marketing directors. 'Keeping up with trends' was the main driver of their use of social media. This scored far higher than any hard evidence, or even gut feel, on the business-building effect of social media (Figure 8.5).

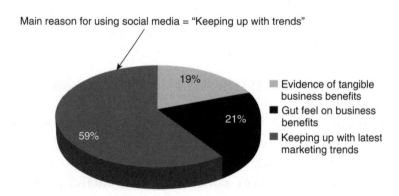

Figure 8.5: Social media is fuelled by fads and fashion.
(Source: brandgym research, 2012).

---

* NOTE: 'social media' here refers to the creation of brand-related content and not to advertising on social media websites

On the plus side, social media are a relatively cheap way of reaching an audience of potential buyers of your brand and so growing the core. The main cost being that of a team to create and curate content. So, it's worth investing some time and money in using them if you can make your presence distinctive and reach a big enough audience. But first, we need to cut through the hype and hysteria, before looking at suggestions on how best to use them to grow the core.

Cutting through the hype

Old media ain't dead yet

Sensationalist, scaremongering messages about the demise of TV advertising are popular headline-grabbers in the media and at conferences. As Byron Sharp comments (10): 'There are plenty of social-media marketing zealots, who say ridiculous things like "TV advertising is dead", many of whom have a vested interest (in social media).' In reality, conventional media still have an important role to play in growing the core. Research on TV advertising in the UK by Thinkbox (4) shows just how powerful TV still is:

- **TV delivers the best ROI:** in an extensive econometric study, TV advertising delivered £1.70 profit per £1 invested, 2.5 times more effective than the next best performing medium, which was press.
- **TV is getting MORE effective:** TV's ROI **increased** by 22% in the last five years, owing to i) reduced price of TV, ii) commercial TV viewing up by 3 hours, 30 minutes a week in the last 10 years.
- **90% of TV is still watched live:** predictions that personal video recorders like Sky+ or TIVO would kill TV advertising by allowing people to record TV programmes and so skip the ads seem to be exaggerated. More than 90% of TV is still watched live.

But what about the power of word-of-mouth, which is now fuelled by social media? Isn't this making conventional media like TV irrelevant? Well, research by Ed Keller and Brad Fay suggests not (11): 'Online social networks are far from the Holy Grail of marketing. A far bigger and more powerful force is real world, face-to-face conversation'. Their research shows that 90% of word-of-mouth conversations about brands still take place offline, primarily face-to-face. Furthermore, the quality of offline word-of-mouth is higher, as they say: 'These conversations bring greater credibility, a greater desire to share with others, and a greater likelihood to purchase the products being discussed than conversations that take place online.' And when conversations do happen, good old-fashioned paid advertising plays a key role. Ed and Brad found that 25% of brand conversations include a specific reference to an advert, saying: 'Far from being a dinosaur, television and other traditional media play a key role in today's social marketplace.' Indeed, many of the most famous examples of viral online success were originally driven by TV advertising. Take one of the most talked about social media campaigns, Old Spice's 'The man your man could smell like', with its 41 million+ views on YouTube. This campaign was ignited with the most conventional form of 'old' media there is: a TV advert in the Superbowl.

Social media have limited reach

Most social media experts suggest social media are about 'engaging' brand users to turn them into extra loyal brand fans. However, as shown earlier in the book, loyalty levels between brands are, in reality, similar. The key to core brand growth is to drive penetration by reaching as many people as possible, especially light and non-users of your brand. And this is the Achilles heel of social media. *Brandgym* research with US and UK consumers shows that 85% of a brand's social media followers were already users of the brand before they started following it.

Social media are a way of potentially amplifying the rest of your communication efforts, rather than replacing them altogether, given the limited role they can play in driving penetration with light and non-users. To get more of an idea about the role social media can play for your core business, we need to look at what sort of brand you have.

Prada or pasta sauce?

One of the biggest problems with social media is companies rushing into them without first asking how appropriate they are for their brand. To start with, let's get real about the role of brands in general in social media. Only 7% of UK people saw social media as being very important for staying in touch and interacting with brands, with the number slightly higher in the US. This is dwarfed by the importance of connecting with friends and family (Figure 8.6). These results help explain why people like, on average, only nine brands on Facebook, compared to an average of 200+ friends.

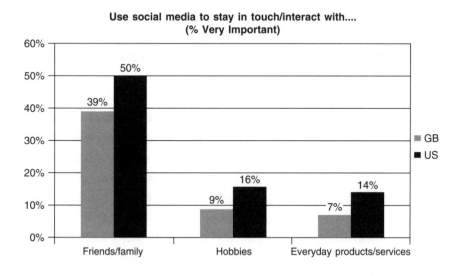

Figure 8.6: Percentage use of social media.

And within this minor role for brands, not all brands are equal. Here's a simple set of three questions to score out of 10 to help you think about your own brand's fit with social media:

1. **How social is your brand?** Is it a 'social' brand, one that forms an important part of people's social life? If social media are a virtual pub or café where conversation happens, would people there talk about your brand? Would people want to read the weekly magazine of your brand, or watch its daily TV show? Now, if you're lucky enough to be marketing a sexy fashion brand, a TV show or sports team brand, then perhaps the answer to these questions is 'yes'. However, if you're working on an everyday brand that is closer to pasta sauce or pet food than Prada, then the answer is probably 'no'. Indeed, research by DDB confirms that consumer goods products are bottom of the list of the average nine brands people like on Facebook (12). At the top of the list were media, fashion, sport and charities. These sorts of brands can create a stream of potential news stories, whereas there is much less to talk about if you're a brand of pasta sauce, pet food or toilet rolls.

    How social is your brand: score/10

2. **How many of your sales are online?** Another key factor that's often overlooked when discussing social media is the link to selling more stuff. If online is a key sales channel for your brand, then social media can play a direct selling role. An example of a brand like this is *The X-Factor*, a reality TV singing contest, similar to *Idols* in other markets. The brand's UK Facebook page had a whopping 3.7million likes during the 2011 season. And social media are not only communication channels, **they're revenue drivers**. They can help *The X-Factor* generate online revenue by people buying iTunes tracks of the week's songs and the Christmas song. Another revenue driver is encouraging mobile phone voting for who stays on the show. In

contrast, for consumer goods brands, the link to selling more of the core is much more indirect. The best an FMCG brand can do is link to an online shopping site, but this is still a niche channel. For example, in the UK, Internet shopping is only 3% of the UK grocery market.

Importance of online selling: score/10

3. **How important are teens and young adults?** Younger people are far bigger users of social media and use them more often. Therefore, for a brand like Lynx/Axe, social media are far more important communication channels. The younger generation has grown up with watching content on YouTube and staying in touch with Facebook and Twitter. In contrast, for a more mainstream brand with a more typical user profile, social media will play a less important role.

Importance of teens/young people: score/10

Total score /30

Now, add up your three scores to get a total. In this highly sophisticated media model, this is the percentage of your time and money to allocate on social media. Here's what the scores might look like for three different brands: *The X-Factor* reality TV show, Lynx/Axe body spray and Kellogg's.

	X-Factor/Idols	Lynx/Axe	Kellogg's
How social?	8	6	2
How online?	5	1	1
How young?	7	9	2
Total/% budget	20	16	5

The *brandgym* social media survey confirmed that social media have a minor, supporting role for most brands. Most marketing directors said that social media would take up less than 5% of their budget (Figure 8.7). The proportion of team time was higher than the percentage of budget, reflecting the

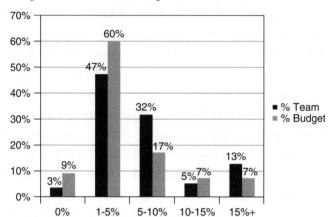

% of budget and team time Marketing Directors allocate to social media

Figure 8.7: Social media take less than 10% of budget and team time.
(Source: brandgym research, 2012).

fact that social media investment is more about talent and time than money.

So, with a clearer idea of the role social media can play in growing the core, let's now look at how to best use the c.5–10% of your time, talent and money you might allocate to them.

Content is king

99% only consume content

The biggest difference with social media compared to 'paid for' media like TV is the importance of content. Content is king. But many marketers seem to fall into the trap of thinking that consumers will create a lot of this content for them. They have been egged on by social media evangelists who claim that mass marketing is being replaced by 'conversations', where people create content in a two-way dialogue with brands.

In fact, far fewer people are interested in two-way interaction, as shown by our *brandgym* research (Figure 8.8). This is backed up by further research by the Ehrenberg-Bass

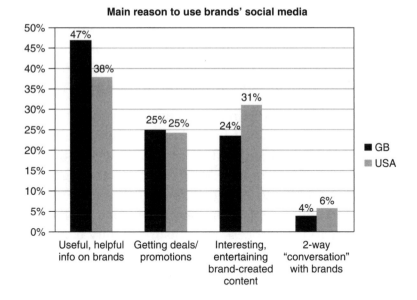

Figure 8.8: Consumers don't want a conversation.
(Source: brandgym research, 2012).

Institute (EBI) on the top 200 brands on Facebook (13). The EBI used a Facebook metric, 'People Talking About This' that adds up the total likes, posts, comments, tags, shares and other ways of interacting with brand pages. On average, only 1.3% of brand page likers were interacting with brand pages.

So, how come 99% of people don't interact with brands on Facebook? First, most of us are simply too busy to bother creating content. Indeed, for many or even most brands, we wouldn't be interested in a conversation at all even if we had time. Ben Hammersley of Wired UK put it this way, in an article in *Marketing* (14) 'The notion that consumers want to take time out of their busy lives to watch content or even co-create it is a myth. Nobody ever wanted to do any of this. People only think of your brand once – when they buy it.' And even if your brand is sexy and/or interesting, most of the people visiting your social media site, such as Facebook or YouTube, are there to consume content, not create it.

A new type of team

The need for a stream of distinctive, relevant content is a big change versus traditional marketing. P&G's branding boss, Marc Pritchard, suggests brand teams today need to act like a 'newsroom', with several important implications (14):

- **Hiring an editor:** creating and 'curating' content is a skill-set most marketers don't have. You may need to hire in or sub-contract to someone with writing or journalistic experience. This person needs to have perfected the right 'voice' in which to write to bring to life the brand personality. Whilst different people can contribute content, the editor needs to lead this process and ensure quality control.

- **Need for speed:** A newsroom is open 24 hours a day and has to react on the spot to important events, as P&G's Pritchard comments: 'You have to organise so you're all co-located. It's not just the client but the agencies. You ask "What's happened in the past 24 hours, how do we need to respond to it?" We get people who are constantly on Twitter, Facebook and all forms of social media.' And speed is not just in terms of content creation, it also includes speed of response to comments from your consumers. At a recent conference, UK retailer Marks & Spencer explained how it works on a two-hour response time to comments in social media.

- **Keep some flex:** given the need for speed of response, you need to be agile when doing social media. Here's Marc Pritchard again: 'You can still plan a lot – 80% of your activities – you just have to be ready for the unplanned activities. This means having some budget and time allocated to be responsive.' Pritchard gives the Olympics as an example: 'We're ready to see how our athletes do, ready to see how our brands do.'

- **Learn by doing:** one key advantage of social media is you can get real-time data on your activities, allowing you to adjust your spend, as Marc Pritchard notes: 'Do things and learn about them. I know if we put a YouTube video out there and it gets 7000 hits in three days, it's a pig! Take it down. Do something else. With Old Spice we knew we had a hit. And then we poured the gas on. We went to our PR people about getting Isaiah Mustafa on talk shows. We ran some more advertising and heavied it up. And so we fuelled the fire.'

- **Hit the headlines:** the key challenge for a newsroom is to have a stream of interesting, impactful news that can make headlines. This is where big service brands have the advantage of a large product range to talk about, in contrast to the limited offer of most product brands. They can also control listing of products, selling what they want and when, including products which are small but newsworthy. For example, UK retailer Marks & Spencer used social media to promote the launch of Percy the Pig ice creams. It sold £100,000 of ice cream in the first month, probably enough to cover the costs of a social media manager for 6 months (15).

There are many different social media platforms you could use; for most companies a bit of focus would help. We will focus the last bit of this chapter on three platforms, based on: i) The size of audience: this is important to get reach and so help drive penetration of the core, ii) brand added value: the opportunity to create distinctive content where the brand has a starring role. Based on these criteria, we'll focus on Facebook, Twitter and YouTube:

- **Facebook** is way ahead of the rest of the crowd. This is based on its huge audience (901 million at the time of writing) and it being the platform with by far the most opportunity for brand added value.
- **Twitter** has a supporting role to play, although this is very different to the lead role played by Facebook, as we will see later. It has much more limited reach, owing to fewer members (300 million) and less brand relevance. This is

shown by the Top 10 brands in the UK having a Twitter following only 1% the size of their Facebook following.

- **YouTube** also has a role to play given its huge audience, with 2 billion views per day (nearly double the prime time audience of the three major US TV networks combined). The platform is obviously more limited than Facebook in terms of branded content and the sort of videos that get viewed are entertainment based, which works for some brands but not for others.

In contrast, some of the newer platforms such as Pinterest have both less reach (c.12 million monthly average users) and also much less opportunity for brands to add value. The same goes for Instagram, which also has limited opportunities for branded content. These very visual platforms may have relevance for a handful of brands that are also visual in nature, such as department stores or fashion brands which can showcase their new collections.

Facebook

As we saw earlier, 99% of people are going to be consuming content, not creating it, on Facebook. The first thing to understand is how they consume this content, as it's not quite how you might imagine.

The newsfeed

As few as 10% of people ever go back to a brand's Facebook page (16). Rather, people consume brand content as part of their 'newsfeed' and this is full of news from friends and family that is much more important than most of the news your brand will be sending them. This means your brand's content has to be truly distinctive and relevant to have a chance of standing out at all.

The second important point about content on Facebook is the growing importance of mobile. In the UK, half of all

Facebook usage is on a mobile device. The figure is even higher in markets where fast broadband has limited availability for PCs, such as South Africa, where mobile makes up 80% of Facebook usage. The implication of this is the need for bite-size bits of news that can be read easily on a mobile device.

Facebook in action: innocent smoothies

A good example of Facebook being used as a form of distinctive communication is UK smoothie brand, innocent. Its Facebook page has over 250,000 likes, pretty high for a UK-focused brand. More importantly, it has the highest level of interaction I have found, with almost 8% of the people liking the page 'talking about it'. This is c. 8 times the average level of interaction of the 200 brands in the EIB survey referenced earlier. Here's how it does this:

Entertaining brand: innocent is an exceptional case of a consumer goods brand that is highly entertaining and social. From the birth of the brand, it has had a publishing approach, creating a stream of entertaining content. This started by using bottle labels as a form of 'packvertising', as covered earlier in the book. It was also one of the first brands to start using blogging and newsletters. It also benefits from having a relatively large range of products, including smoothies, smoothies for kids and veg pots, and a long-term strategy of limited edition products. This gives the brand plenty of product news to talk about.

In-house creative team: innocent has always invested in having amazing in-house creative resource. A team of 15 people is led by creative supremo Dan Germain. This means the company really does have a newsroom full of writers able to create compelling, distinctive content.

Short, sharp and visual: a quick look at innocent's Facebook feed is enough to see it is following the golden rules to get into the newsfeed detailed above. The brand's posts are short, sharp, interactive and highly visual. Here's a taste of what they were posting about as I was writing this page:

- Funny pictures of animals;
- Winner of the design a bottle competition;
- New kids' smoothie flavour;
- How rainy days help make conversation;
- Olympic medals for everyday achievements.

YouTube

Every marketing director's dream is to have a YouTube sensation that 'goes viral'. And a viral video does provide additional exposure for the core brand's communication. However, a reality check is needed on the role YouTube really can play for most brands.

The viral lottery

The first big challenge with YouTube is that it's a 'viral lottery'. Few adverts ever go viral and so get any decent exposure. And to make things worse, what works and what doesn't work is very hard to predict. For example, UK yoghurt brand Yeo Valley hit the headlines with an advert featuring rapping farmers back in December 2010. Most of the brand's advertising budget was spent on a single advert break during one of the UK's biggest TV programmes, *The X-Factor*. However, what gets less press coverage, of course, is the multitude of adverts that don't go viral. Indeed, taking a look at the YouTube views for other yoghurt brands shows that the Yeo Valley farmers' 2.5 million views was something of a one-off. The follow-up TV advert, Churned Forever, got less than a third of these views. And most other yoghurt adverts have much lower figures (Figure 8.9).

Un-plannable

The second big issue with YouTube viral videos is that the audience is completely un-targeted. Even if yours is one of

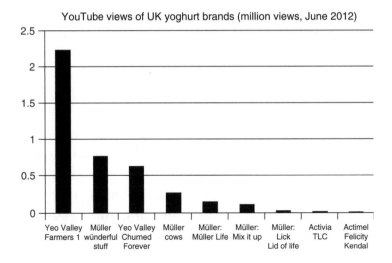

Figure 8.9: The viral video lottery.
(Source: YouTube).

the handful of videos that goes viral, unlike TV advertising, you have no way of planning where those million views
will come from. What age? Which socio-demographic group?
Which country? The same people lots of times or lots of
people only once? In the earlier case of Yeo Valley, a lot of
the advertising budget was blown on a single, highly expensive advert to 'ignite' an online viral explosion. This reduced
the TV exposure to yoghurt shoppers in return for YouTube
viewing by an audience that can't be controlled. Those rapping farmers may have been watched more by kids who
liked it when they saw the ad in *The X-Factor*, rather than
by the busy mums who actually buy yoghurt. This may be
why interviews with industry sources suggest that the Yeo
Valley campaign got plenty of YouTube exposure but didn't
do much for market share, which is, in fact, down.

Sex, smiles and spectacle
The final challenge for using YouTube to grow the core is
that what you need to go viral may not fit with your brand

positioning. The three key things that seem to drive viral videos, with the emphasis on 'seem', are the 3 S's:

- Sex: anything that is raunchy and sexy is likely to be viewed a lot. This works well if you are Lynx/Axe, a brand producing videos verging on soft porn!
- Smiles: above all, funny videos are the ones which go viral. A good example is the series of 'flash mob' and spoof videos done by T-Mobile (people dancing in a train station, singing at airport arrivals, karaoke in Trafalgar Square).
- Spectacle: videos which are amazing, impressive, cinematic, have a 'wow' factor. For example, the Hovis re-make of its Boy on a Bike advert from earlier in the chapter.

As mentioned, the challenge is to do something with one of all of the three S's, and yet be authentic to your brand. In addition, another major challenge is to do this and not just create 'sponsored entertainment': an entertaining film where the only role of the brand is a logo slapped at the end. To be distinctive and help create brand awareness that can drive penetration, the brand needs to play a starring role.

Perhaps the best example of this is Tippex's 'Bear and a Hunter' video. This consisted of a face-to-face encounter between the bear and hunter where the viewer is offered the opportunity to choose the ending they want. This video had an impressive 40 million views on YouTube, and the creators of the campaign claim it has helped double purchase intent and increased sales by 30% in Europe (13). Even pop star Ricky Martin tweeted about the ad to his millions of followers.

- Branded: the brand is cleverly embedded into the video by the hunter using the Tippex to white-out the word 'shoots', and asking the viewer to type in a new word. There are a multitude of different words which work, including the obvious.

- Smiles and spectacle (and a bit of sex): the video is very funny and has a sense of spectacle through the interactivity (and the odd naked lady thrown in for fun).
- Fit with target: students are a key target for Tippex, so there is a good fit with the YouTube channel.

For most brands, especially everyday consumer goods brands, I suggest that going viral should be seen as the 'cherry on the cake': a bonus beyond your 'bought media'. The reason for this is that viral videos are hard to predict, impossible to plan and difficult to do with the three S's whilst being on brand. Word-of-mouth chat down the pub about your new advert worked in this way before social media. All the new technology does is create a new way for great marketing to be amplified.

Twitter

Tiny Twitter

Twitter is much less important as a channel for direct brand communication. US research by Chadwick Martin via Mashable Business shows that only 21% of people follow any brands at all. Of these, only 36% follow more than four (16). In other words, only 7% of people are following more than four brands on Twitter. Our own brandgym research shows that Twitter following is roughly 1% the level of Facebook following, based on the UK's top 10 brands. This makes sense, as people sign up to Facebook brand pages which have a much more interesting content in the form of fun and entertaining news, games and competitions. In contrast, Twitter is more about short, 140-character soundbites, and so the opportunity for brand communication is clearly limited. Not many brands have a stream of bit-sized news stories that make them worth following, as comedian Ross Noble pointed out in a hilarious sketch:

> Why has Doritos got their own Twitter feed?! What can they say? They're still cheesy. They're still cheesy, again. So we bombarded

them with thousands of stupid questions like 'I have a much-loved family moth that's injured its wing. Could you use a Dorito as a replacement wing?'

So, given its limitations, how can it be used by brands?

Helpline

One role for Twitter is to be a new form of helpline. It is funny how there has never been a queue of marketing folk wanting to man the phone helplines, nor open and reply to consumer letters or emails. Now it's called social media, they're all over it. Using Twitter as a helpline is especially relevant for complex service brands where stuff goes wrong, or where there are lots of questions. The great thing about using Twitter in this way is the possibility of showing some sort of ROI by demonstrating the reduction in costs from cutting down on helplines. Also, in some cases Twitter is much more effective. For example, my brother works for a local council which has found it to be highly effective at finding homes for stray dogs. On a bigger level, US retailer Best Buy uses a 'Tweepforce' to reply to customer questions and enquiries.

Celebrity CEOs

Twitter is, on the whole, about personal communication. Thank goodness people are more interested in Twitter updates from celebrities, sports stars and friends than from bread and bog rolls. This is why most brands have a limited Twitter following. The one exception to this is brands that have celebrity CEOs. For example, 2.1 million people are following the Tweets of Virgin's Sir Richard Branson. This is over 10 times the number following British Airways. A whopping 2.4 million follow the CEO of US retailer Zappos, Tony Hsieh. This is almost 200 times the following of Zappos.com at 13 000.

A good example of what not to do with Twitter is to try and invent celebrity status for your products like the Greggs brand of stores in the UK. Greggs's CEO, Ken McMeikan, pushed the story that the creation of Twitter profiles for each of the new range of doughnuts they launched (e.g. @coconut snowball) played a key role in their successful launch. He told reporters: 'Through social media marketing we gave each of the doughnuts their own voice where they were talking about themselves and interacting with fans.' However, it's hard to see how a Twitter following of c. 800 people per doughnut can have done much to shift the 1.4 million doughnuts sold in the first five weeks of the launch!

Focus on great marketing

As mentioned before, people always talked about great marketing. And Twitter is just one more way to do this. The benefit of Twitter is that TV news shows and journalists now use it as a source of sound-bite quotes. Why bother interviewing a celebrity for a quote when you can just use their Tweets? So, if you make your brand mix interesting enough, you might be lucky enough to have someone famous Tweet about you. Or, more likely, you may have users of your brand who Tweet about you to their friends and family. But as with YouTube, I suggest this is the cherry on the cake of your core brand marketing mix.

 Key takeouts

1. To be effective at growing the core, communication needs to deliver fresh consistency.
2. Consistency comes from both a unifying brand story and the creation and amplification of distinctive brand properties that create memory structure.

3. Freshness comes from updating the execution and bringing news in the form of chapters of marketing activity.

 ## Checklist 8. Communicate with cut-through

	Yes	No
• Have you got a clear brand story that can work to create consistency across your chapters of communication?	☐	☐
• Do your briefs for advertising talk about the importance of creating and amplifying distinctive brand properties to build memory structure?	☐	☐
• Have you evaluated the role social media can play for your brand, before spending too much time and money on them?	☐	☐

 ## Handover

You have now seen how distinctive communication can help create memory structure and so drive penetration to grow the core. Now you will move onto the last of the four ways to create distinctive marketing, by seeing how to go beyond promotions to brand activation.

Headlines

Most promotional activity on brands is predictable and not linked to the brand idea, such as money-off deals or offering extra product for free. However, done well, brand activation can play an important role in making the core brand more distinctive and so help drive penetration. This starts with understanding the 'passion points' of the target audience and identifying which are relevant and linked to both the brand story and the product usage occasion. Then, the challenge is to go beyond simply adding the brand's logo to the event or activity, by creating a distinctive activation property. This property then needs to be amplified both over the mix and over time, in order to create memory structure.

Scan a shelf of your local supermarket for promotional offers and you're unlikely to find much in the way of creativity. It's probably full of 'buy one get one free' (BOGOF) and '25% off' promotions. Perhaps there will be the odd offer to enter a competition and 'Win a Holiday' or some similar prize. These promotions might have a short-term effect on sales, but they do little to really drive distinctiveness and so increase penetration for the core.

In contrast, 'brand activation' goes beyond promotion to boost sales as it works harder at communicating the brand idea in a distinctive and memorable way. If the activation idea is amplified consistently over the mix and over time, it has the potential to become a distinctive brand property that can help create memory structure for the brand. One of the leading brands in this field is Red Bull. It has identified a series of high-adrenalin sports with appeal to its target audience of young, active men. The genius is then in the way Red Bull creates and amplifies distinctive properties for each of these, such as The Red Bull Air Race in aerobatic flying and Red Bull X-Fighters for stunt motorcycling. In each case, the activation property literally brings to life the brand idea of 'Gives you Wings'. These properties also help Red Bull create a distinctive memory structure in a way that is more powerful, authentic and exciting than using advertising alone.

Brand activation has two advantages over conventional promotions: grabbing attention and bringing to life the brand story. We'll explore these two benefits using the example of innocent smoothies' Big Knit brand activation.

Grab and go – innocent's Big Knit

innocent smoothies' Big Knit activation has been part of the marketing that has helped innocent grow the core smoothie business from nothing to a brand with £100 million in sales in just 10 years. Until recently, this growth was achieved without significant advertising support.

Grabbing attention

Around wintertime, something interesting happens to the smoothies section of UK supermarkets, which grabs your attention (Figure 9.1). The little bottles of innocent smoothies, the leading brand in the sector, are wearing cute little woolly hats. Each one has a different design. Look closer and you can find out that each special woolly hat bottle you buy raises 50p for the Help the Aged charity to help protect old people from the cold. Here, we see the first advantage of brand activation, which is to make your brand more distinctive and so stand out on shelf.

Bringing to life the brand story

The Big Knit also helps bring to life the innocent brand's caring side, by dramatising the brand's support for a good cause.

Figure 9.1: An activation property that stands out on shelf. Reproduced by permission of Innocent Drinks.

Importantly, innocent doesn't just stick the hats on the bottles and leave it at that. The activation is amplified across the mix, especially through the use of innocent's digital marketing programme, involving the website, email newsletter, blog and social media channels. Consumers are actively involved through an invitation to help knit the little woolly hats themselves. Progress towards the target is tracked via a 'Hatometer'. This amplification has helped innocent increase the number of hats knitted from 20 000 in 2003 to a whopping 650 000 in 2011. The activation has, in total, helped raise £1 million for charity.

Other activation ideas reinforce this idea of being a caring brand by communicating the innocent brand's charitable work, part of an approach it calls 'FMSG': Fast Moving Sustainable Goods. The brand even had a clever play on the boring BOGOF (buy one get one free) called 'Buy One Get One TREE'. This promotion invited people to buy a one litre carton of innocent and, in return, the brand planted a tree for you in Africa. You were able to visit a virtual forest on the innocent website where you could enter your name and see the tree you had helped fund.

Let's now move on to look in more detail at how to create your own distinctive activation property.

Creating an activation property – Carling 'Be the Coach'

Creating a distinctive activation property requires a different approach to your run-of-the-mill brainstorming. Rather than launching into idea creation, the approach starts with identifying an activation insight you can build on. This is then the springboard for creating the distinctive activation property itself.

We'll work through this approach using one of the most exciting examples of brand activation I've been lucky enough to work on: the Carling Black Label's 'Be the Coach' campaign from SAB Miller in South Africa. The activation generated an impressive 11 million entries in seven weeks. It has helped revitalise the brand and was winner of the best global mobile marketing award in 2011.

Tap into passion points

The start point for activation idea generation is to identify 'passion points': things that your target consumer is interested in. In the case of Carling Black Label, the team identified and then explored a number of different passion points including soccer, rugby, music and technology. Each passion point was brought to life, looking at aspirational brands and the emotions attached to it. Then the passion points were reviewed using three main criteria: relevance, link to the brand story and link to usage occasions (Figure 9.2).

1. Relevance

All the passion points were relevant to some degree to the target audience, but of these, one stuck out in particular. Soccer is by far the most popular sport in South Africa

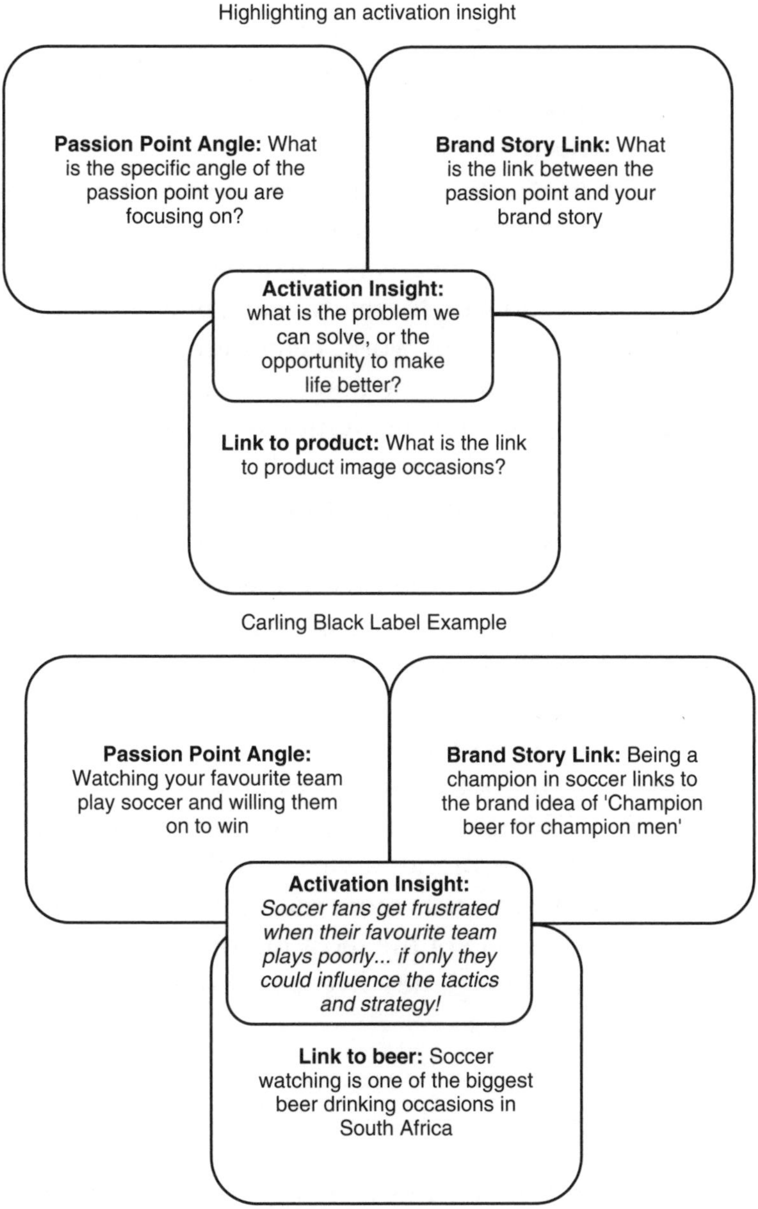

Highlighting an activation insight

Passion Point Angle: What is the specific angle of the passion point you are focusing on?

Brand Story Link: What is the link between the passion point and your brand story

Activation Insight: what is the problem we can solve, or the opportunity to make life better?

Link to product: What is the link to product image occasions?

Carling Black Label Example

Passion Point Angle: Watching your favourite team play soccer and willing them on to win

Brand Story Link: Being a champion in soccer links to the brand idea of 'Champion beer for champion men'

Activation Insight: *Soccer fans get frustrated when their favourite team plays poorly... if only they could influence the tactics and strategy!*

Link to beer: Soccer watching is one of the biggest beer drinking occasions in South Africa

Figure 9.2: Highlighting an activation insight.

and, in particular, the team identified club soccer as a specific aspect of soccer to tap into. This enabled the brand to be distinctive versus another key SAB Miller brand, Castle Lager, which was already activating around the national South African sports teams.

2. Link to brand story

Having identified a series of passion points, the next step is to overlay the brand story you are trying to tell. For Carling Black Label, the brand idea was 'Champion Beer for Champion Men'. The brand had, for many years, been positioned as a reward for hard physical work, celebrating the blue-collar worker. However, in the new South Africa physical labourers were no longer seen as aspirational role models. Hence, from 2010 onwards, the brand sought to re-define its portrayal of masculinity from being about working-class heroes to a more contemporary and multi-faceted expression of masculine achievement. With the Champion idea in mind, it was easy to see that passion points in the area of sport had a natural fit and would be easier to use in bringing to life the brand idea.

3. Link to usage occasions

The third thing to look at is how to link the activation to a usage occasion. This gives the activation a relevant 'context', where the link to the brand is clear. In the case of Carling Black Label, sport again was more relevant than, say, technology or cars. Sport is one of the most important beer-drinking occasions – watching games live and especially watching sport on TV with mates.

Activation insight

To create an activation property that is distinctive, we need to go beyond a general passion point. We need to dig deeper to find a specific angle we can take. For Carling Black Label, the specific angle identified was the way guys get frustrated at what they see as bad coaching decisions in soccer matches.

They spend hours debating who should play and not play and shout at the TV or at the game when things go wrong. This led to the activation insight 'I get frustrated at not being able to influence team selection . . . if only I could have a more active role in helping my team win.'

Distinctive brand property

Having identified the insight around wanting to influence the team's fortunes, the brand team and creative agencies, Ogilvy and Brandtone, then worked on how to deliver against this. The ambition was to go beyond simple 'logo slapping', where brands sponsor a sports event or team, for example Budweiser sponsoring the World Cup. Here, the brand gets limited benefit beyond brand awareness, and perhaps some image benefit from association with the sports brand. In contrast, Carling Black Label created an activation property, 'Be the Coach', which is more distinctive and so more likely to create memory structure (Figure 9.3). This required the brand to add real value, not just its brand name.

Be the Coach involved taking consumer interactivity to a whole new level. It allowed soccer fans to actually vote

Figure 9.3: Creating an activation property. Reproduced by permission of SAB Miller plc.

and pick the teams for a special cup match between South Africa's top two teams, the Kaiser Chiefs and The Orlando Pirates. Both these teams are based in Johannesburg, giving the match an extra dimension of being a 'local derby'. Fans were able to select a player in a preferred position via USSD (a form of text messaging). This made the promotion available to many more South Africans than if it had been done via PC. The mechanism was kept simple to maximise the number of entries.

In a clever move, participants then heard from the coaches of the teams via pre-recorded messages. Then, during the actual match, watched by 80 000 in the stadium and millions on TV, fans actually got to vote via mobile for a live substitution!

This idea really brought to life the brand story of Champion Beer for Champion Men. First, the winner of the cup was, of course, the champion team, and so Carling is the beer of champions. Secondly, and more importantly, the ability to vote and be the coach made brand drinkers feel like they were champions themselves.

Amplification

Importantly, the property was amplified in the build-up to the actual cup itself in July. This meant the brand got maximum effect from the idea, beyond the people who attended the event. The innovative nature of the idea meant it got a lot of PR coverage, valued at c. £8 million. The issue of amplification is an important one, so we'll now look at it in more detail using the example of Nike.

Amplifying the property – Nike

To have maximum effect in creating distinctiveness for the core brand, the activation property needs to be amplified in two key ways: first over the marketing mix, before, during and after the activation itself. This is key to ensure that the activation has an impact beyond those people who actively participate in it. Second, the idea needs to be amplified over time to help create memory structure.

Amplification over the mix

For a brand activation to have the biggest possible impact, the idea needs to be amplified across the mix to broaden its reach beyond the people who actually participate in the event or activity. I got some valuable insights into how to do this by talking to Ed Elworthy, Nike's Global Communication Director for Soccer. Ed talked me through the example of an activation called 'Show Your 5'. This was a National five-a-side soccer tournament, designed to 'Give young players a platform to express themselves positively through urban football'. The activation had 26 000 players participating in 200 tournaments over eight weeks, divided into seven regions. Local winning teams went through to city finals and eventually the national final. The idea was to tap into the more gritty, edgy world of urban football played in inner cities. The key to the amplification of Show Your 5 was doing this before, during and after the activity itself, to build up the level of noise around it:

– Before:

- Content from the TV ad, which featured soccer stars like Wayne Rooney playing with city teenagers, was seeded on the Internet and with soccer bloggers.
- A 30-second teaser of the ad was released on the Internet. It gained a high level of YouTube views, helped by the fact that it showed one of the teenagers 'nutmegging' Wayne Rooney: kicking the ball through his legs.
- The activation was launched with an ad during the Champions League Final.

– **During:**

- Outdoor, press and digital channels were used to get people to create their own teams and sign up to the competition.

– **After:**

- Adverts at the stadium drove people to Nike.com to watch the highlights of the match.
- An ongoing partnership with urban five-a-side football was designed to have some form of positive 'legacy' from the activation.

Amplification over time

One of the key principles of growing the core is creating fresh consistency and this applies one hundred per cent to brand activation. Many brand teams seek to re-invent the marketing plan every year. This is based on a misplaced belief that consumers will be bored after one exposure to a marketing programme. In reality, I suggest that marketing teams get bored a lot more quickly than consumers. They feel the need for novelty, but in doing so create so much change that nothing is really remembered. To recap, memory structure takes an estimated two to three years to establish.

Rather than start from scratch each year, growing the core through activation involves taking an activation property and applying the principle of fresh consistency. A good example of this is Nike's 'Run London' activation, which ran for seven years from 2001 to 2008 (1). The consistent elements were a race with mass participation and some form of personal challenge. Freshness was added by bringing a clever twist to the activation, to make each year bigger and better than the last, with the result that more people participated.

— 2001: Run London – 10 000 runners
— 2004: Run at night – 30 000 runners

— 2006: North vs. South – 35 000 runners

— 2008: Run the world – global event with 780 000 runners

For example, the third version of the activation was called 'North vs. South'. This tapped into a long-standing rivalry between people living north and south of the River Thames in London. Posters for the activation announced: 'North vs. South. Let's Settle It Once and For All'. You signed up for the event to represent your side of the river and got a running vest in the colour of your team: green for north, yellow for south. You also got a micro-chip for your shoes linked to your team. Not only did you then get a personal time for running, your time also contributed to your team. The side that recorded the overall best time (from the collected times of all the individual runners in each team) was declared the winner. I'm happy to say that the winner was the south, the part of London where I live!

The last event in 2008 took things to a whole new level by turning it into 'Run the World'. Here, runners represented their country, not just their city. This was the world's largest running event with nearly 780 000 participants. I love the way the introduction to this activation sums up the idea of fresh consistency, by recapping the history of the event:

You ran at night
You ran a year
You ran for your side of the river
Now it's time to take your 10k global
Race the world on Aug 31, 2008.

 Key takeouts

1. Brand activation goes beyond classic promotions, being more impactful and playing an active role in bringing to life the brand idea.

2. Brand activation involves identifying a passion point that is relevant to your target consumer and linked to both the brand idea and the context in which the product or service is consumed.

3. Rather than just logo slapping, the brand activation should create a distinctive brand property which is amplified over the mix and over time.

Checklist 9. Go beyond promotion to activity

	Yes	No
• Have you identified a passion point that is relevant to your target consumer and linked to both the brand idea and product usage?	☐	☐
• Rather than just logo slapping, have you created a distinctive activation property?	☐	☐
• Do you have a plan to amplify this activation property over the mix and over time?	☐	☐

Handover

You have now seen how to use distinctive activation properties to make your core brand more salient and so drive penetration. This completes the four ways of making the brand more distinctive. You will discover how distribution can also be used to drive penetration and grow the core.

Workouts 5 and 6: Drive your distribution

CHAPTER 10

DISTINCTIVENESS

PENETRATION

GROW THE CORE

PREMIUMISATION

EXTENSION

DISTRIBUTION

1. PRODUCT

2. IDENTITY

3. COMMS

4. ACTIVATION

5. EXISTING CHANNELS

6. NEW CHANNELS

7. PACK EXTENSION

8. PRODUCT EXTENSION

Headlines

Driving distribution of the core is one of the most effective ways of increasing penetration by reaching more people, more often. The first way to do this is to increase the brand's presence in existing channels, both in terms of number of outlets and the presence instore through multiple sitings. A bolder approach with bigger, long-term benefits is to open up new routes to the consumer. This has the advantage of giving brands back some of the power they have lost to the major retailers.

Distribution isn't the sexiest bit of marketing. However, whilst neither I nor anyone else have any idea whether your sexy, social-media campaign will sell more stuff, I'd bet my life savings that being sold in more places definitely will. Extending distribution increases the number of consumers you can reach, and so it's an excellent way of driving penetration of the core.

The challenge with distribution for consumer goods brands is, of course, the ever-increasing power of the big retailers. In the UK, the Big Four supermarkets (Tesco, Sainsbury's, Asda and Morrisons) account for almost 80% of all grocery products bought (1). In the USA, Wal-Mart is a $250 billion monster, wielding incredible power over brand owners. This is why the 'route to the consumer' is one of the key challenges for brands in the coming years, if not the biggest one.

To grow the core through distribution there are two main routes you can use: the first is extending your distribution in existing channels; the second route is opening up new channels. This latter approach is more challenging, but in the long term holds bigger benefits for your core brand and business.

Workout 5: Existing channels

The first place to start when trying to grow the core by extending distribution is to work with the existing channels where your brand is sold. In the case of most consumer goods brands, these are the big supermarkets. Here, there are two different ways of increasing presence in existing channels: more is more and multiple sitings. Some of the ideas here will sound simple or even basic, however, in the world of modern marketing these basics are sometimes forgotten, so there's no harm in being reminded of them.

More is more

The most basic way to grow your distribution is simply to extend your brand's presence with existing customers. This has worked wonders for Charlie Bigham's, a fast-growing brand of premium, chilled ready meals. Until Tom Allchurch took over as CEO in 2010, the brand had been sold only in Waitrose' one of the most upscale retailers in the UK. Waitrose had a great fit with the Bigham's brand, with a skew to the urban, upscale foodie consumers the brand appealed to most. However, the issue with sales being only in Waitrose was the limited reach of this retailer, as it only has a 5% share of UK grocery sales. Following a re-launch of the brand with improved products, an extended range and new pack design, Tom and his team worked hard to persuade Sainsbury's to stock the brand. This retailer also has a high proportion of upscale foodie shoppers, but not quite as upscale as Waitrose. It has an excellent reputation for fresh, tasty and high-quality food and, most importantly, it reaches a lot people, having a 16% share of the UK market. This was forecast to dramatically increase the sales of Bigham's by c. 70%.

Clearly getting these sorts of distribution gains is far from easy. So, what are some of the ways brands can help increase their chances of keeping the distribution they have and making distribution gains? Here are some suggestions:

- Focus on the core: retailers are getting more and more ruthless when it comes to smaller brands in a category. Leader Brands have enough consumer 'pull' to justify being stocked, in addition to own-label. However, smaller follower brands are prime targets for de-listing. This means brands need to focus efforts on their core business where the brand has strength in terms of sales and brand equity.
- Build memory structure: talking to retailers, they begrudgingly accept that certain Leader Brands play a key role in 'sign-posting' a category – they help the shopper feel at ease and navigate their way round the shelf. For example, Hellmann's in mayonnaise, Walkers/Lays in potato chips and Kellogg's in breakfast cereals. These brands have incredibly strong brand identities that in the best cases have become iconic.
- Marketing muscle: focusing on the core and creating distinctive marketing helps create 'pull', which makes your brand a must-stock item for retailers. This is why applying the principles of growing the core should help your brand maintain and grow distribution.
- Category leadership: most big consumer goods companies have invested heavily in category management, understanding not just their brand, but the category as a whole. This understanding can be used to show the retailer how your brand is not only growing its own sales, but also sales of the category as a whole.
- Optimise your range: optimising your range can help make the most of the distribution you have. This involves a simple bit of analysis to looking at rate-of-sale by product or pack format in the range, compared to weighted distribution. This highlights products which are selling well, but in relative terms are 'under-distributed', and others where the reverse is true: too much distribution, given the rate of sale. Adjusting the distribution to favour the faster-selling products can help you sell more stuff, and help the retailer make better use of its shelf space.

Table 10.1: Different Coke formats to increase in-store sitings

Format	Price per ml	Price index
– 4 x 2L PET bottles	5.7 p	100
– 6-pack of 33cl cans	11.9 p	208
– 6-pack of 33cl PET bottles	16.3 p	286
– Chilled single bottles in vending machines, for immediate consumption	17.6 p	310

Multiple sitings

The second main way of using existing channels to help grow the core is to make use of multiple sitings. Coca-Cola is the master of this approach. In a typical supermarket the brand is sold in four different places through the use of different product formats (Table 10.1). This approach means that the brand has dramatically extended its reach within a given store and so increased its chances of being seen by the consumer. Notice also the huge difference in pricing, with the most expensive format being sold at three times the price per ml of the cheapest.

Workout 6: New channels

The second main approach to using distribution to grow the core is to open up new routes to consumer. This tends to be much harder, requiring a change to the company's whole business model. This is why, in many cases, channel innovation is discussed at length but limited progress is made. It stays stuck in the 'too difficult' box. However, creating new routes to the market can be an excellent way of growing the core, and a way for brand owners to wrestle back some of the power currently held by the major retailers which have become increasingly dominant over brand owners in the following ways:

• They have become masters at copying branded products and selling them at lower prices. This has got worse with the recession.

- They charge high fees to get listed and there is the constant threat of being booted out if you don't keep 'supporting' the retailer with investment.
- They control in-store pricing.
- They own valuable data on shopper behaviour.

Vending

Mastery of distribution and channels is perhaps the key factor in Coca-Cola's success. They are the experts at getting their brand 'within arm's reach of desire' through different channels, including cafés, hotels and restaurants (CHR) and, of course, vending. The company is continuing to innovate in this channel to grow the core. For example, new vending machines that Coca-Cola has been trialling in Ireland sell not only Coke but a range of other services including ringtones and top-up vouchers for mobile phones. The machine also acts as a digital music jukebox, updated remotely to be always up to date, and can burn CDs (2). The trial of 200 machines has been positive, with revenue per machine twice as high as normal machines. The *Sunday Times* reported that if these results were repeated on the top 10% of Coke's 2.8 million vending machines (accepted this is a bit of a leap), revenue would be boosted by a staggering $1.5 billion (3). What a great way to grow the core.

This approach is also being used by other consumer goods brands, such as the Cup-a-Soup brand in Holland. For many years, Cup-a-Soup was a dormant brand in The Netherlands. Sales of this dehydrated packet soup were static. The brand felt out-dated in a world where the most exciting innovation was happening in chilled food and certainly not dehydrated convenience products. A change in strategy was the catalyst for a period of sustained growth. Same product. Same pack. No radical innovation. The core business was grown by finding and activating a completely new route to market: in offices.

Like many cases of effective marketing, the Cup-a-Soup success started with consumer insight. In this case, the insight was that people in offices experienced an afternoon 'dip' in energy – after a day of coffee and tea, they wanted a different sort of hot 'pick-me-up'. This was a need that Cup-a-Soup was well positioned to capitalise on. It was nourishing, warm and consumers of the product talked of how it had a reviving effect. Unilever Netherlands then did a fantastic job of acting on this insight to create core brand growth:

1. **In-office distribution**: the first task was clearly to get the brand into offices. What was neat about the Cup-a-Soup solution was the cost-effective and quick way it was achieved. Rather than relying on complex vending machines, simple dispensing devices were created, which delivered a portion of Cup-a-Soup that people could pour into their own cups and add boiling water.
2. **The four o'clock break**: Cup-a-Soup cleverly created and sought to own a specific moment of the day – 'the four o'clock break'. This was much more memorable and impactful than just saying 'Drink Cup-a-Soup at work'.
3. **Great communication**: the final piece of the puzzle was using communication to activate the break idea. A tongue-in-cheek campaign featuring the funny, fictional character, John the Office Manager, was created and ran for several years.

Own stores

One of the most impressive examples of a brand using new channels to drive penetration of the core business is Apple. Back in 2001 the company decided to open its first store, with the impetus for this bold move being a frustration with the poor way Apple computers were presented and demonstrated in existing channels. Another key driver for the move into retail was the desire to drive penetration of the core business, as shown by this quote from the company (4): 'One of the goals of the retail initiative is to bring new customers to the company and expand its installed base through sales to computer users who currently do not own a Macintosh computer, and first-time personal computer buyers'. The stores have more than exceeded the expectations on this objective. A whacking 50% of people buying in an Apple store are new to the brand.

Back in 2001 almost all retail analysts were sceptical about Apple's chances of success. How wrong can you be? Here are just a few facts to show how successful Apple has been in opening up this new route to the consumer (5):

- 363 stores worldwide as of January 2012.
- Annual revenue of $17.6 billion, more than JC Penney and nearly as much as Kohl's, both of which have more than three times the number of (considerably larger) stores in the US.
- Average sales per square foot of $6,116, more than twice that of closest rival Tiffany & Co ($3,008) and over 17 times that of the average American mall store ($350).

Steve Jobs avoided the mistake that has tripped up many brands' attempts to get into retailing, which is lack of real retail expertise. Apple did not just want a showcase for its products, it wanted to run the Apple stores as a proper business. To run the stores Jobs brought in Ron Johnson from Target in 2000, and Mickey Drexler, the CEO of Gap, was drafted onto Apple's board.

From the start, the Apple stores didn't look, feel or work like any store that had come before. The stores delivered a totally new customer experience, designed to sell product but also to drive interest in and penetration of the core business. Here are some of the key features that have made them so successful (4):

- Award-winning architecture: open, airy, minimalist, bright.
- Merchandise is displayed in 'solution zones' for hands-on, real-world use.

- A sit-down theatre (benches or chairs) area for instruction, demonstrations and events.
- A 'Genius Bar' where customers can ask questions and solve technical problems. A *Macworld* magazine survey found 34% of those with problems took them to an Apple store Genius Bar.
- An open wireless network, so visitors can bring in their laptops and download e-mail.

Online stores

There are a growing number of brands experimenting with creating their own online stores. Domino's Pizza has increased its share of business done via online ordering. It was one of the first companies to open up this channel, starting back in 1999. Online sales are now reported to make up a whopping 47% of sales, up from 40% a year ago (6). The online figures have been boosted by the recent launch of a new iPad application, which already makes up 13% of e-commerce sales.

Consumer product companies are also experimenting with new online channels. For example, Gillette offers a 'subscription service' to get replacement razors sent to your home. This approach has several advantages:

1. There are loads of guys, like me, who are too lazy to change their blades often enough. The subscription service addresses this.
2. Blunt blades shave less well. By encouraging people to renew blades more often, this should increase consumer satisfaction through a superior shave.
3. This allows Gillette to build a database of consumers and so have direct contact with them.
4. Gillette can control pricing.
5. The company doesn't have to pay the retailer a margin or listing fees or promotional support.
6. It encourages shavers to stick with Gillette and not switch.

The challenge with mono-brand stores is having sufficient products of a high enough value to make the store an interesting place to visit and make it economically viable. This is why Gillette's owner P&G is also experimenting with online retailing to sell its range of brands direct to the consumer. P&G has expanded theessentials.com, an online store set up by Gillette to sell spares for its electrical brands, such as Oral B and Braun. Since buying Gillette, P&G has added its other brands to the site and now people buying spares also have a chance to buy other P&G brands. Whilst this is never going to be a huge business when the range is limited, P&G gets access to interesting data on shoppers, and the chance to do targeted direct marketing and online research. The site is run by a third party and so doesn't take up valuable management time.

The seriousness with which P&G takes online retailing is shown by it taking a 1% share in fast-growing, UK online grocery retailer Ocado. Again, this gives access to valuable insight on shopper behaviour and allows the company to learn more about online retailing. For the relatively small sum of £5 million, P&G gets a share of what could, one day, be a valuable business.

Fish where the fish are

One way of increasing distribution in the core is to look at channels where the category as a whole is not sold at all, but where there is a high concentration of category shoppers. Heinz has taken this approach on two different fronts, selling barbecue sauces at Wyevale Garden Centres and selling baby food in Mothercare. The other day I bought a Costa coffee not from a high-street coffee shop, but from a new dispenser in a service station (Figure 10.1). This follows the purchase of on-the-go, self-service coffee company, Coffee Nation, by Costa's owner Whitbread. The company's CEO Andy Harrison summed up perfectly how this move can help Costa grow

Figure 10.1: New routes to the consumer.

the core by boosting penetration: 'This acquisition provides an exciting launchpad to develop 3000 Costa Express bars across the UK, providing an additional growth lever for the Costa brand and making Costa available to more customers in more locations'.

These moves have several advantages:

• Extend your reach to drive penetration;
• Present the brand in the right environment to reinforce the brand values;
• Create a bit of surprise;
• Promote your brand without competitive clutter.

 Key takeouts

1. Driving distribution of the core is one of the most effective ways of increasing penetration.
2. The first way to do this is to increase the brand's presence in existing channels, both in terms of number of outlets and presence instore, through multiple sitings.

3. A bolder approach with bigger, long-term benefits is to open up new routes to the consumer.

 ## Checklist 10. Drive distribution

	Yes	No
• Have you identified opportunities for increasing your brand's distribution in existing channels?	☐	☐
• Have you worked on increasing presence in store, through multiple sitings?	☐	☐
• Have you considered the possibility of opening up new routes to the consumer through new channels?	☐	☐

 ## Handover

You have now seen the first six workouts for ways of driving penetration, by harnessing both distinctive marketing and increased distribution in existing and new channels. The final two drivers of growth on the core will show you how to extend the core with new formats and products.

Workouts 7 and 8: Extend the core

CHAPTER 11

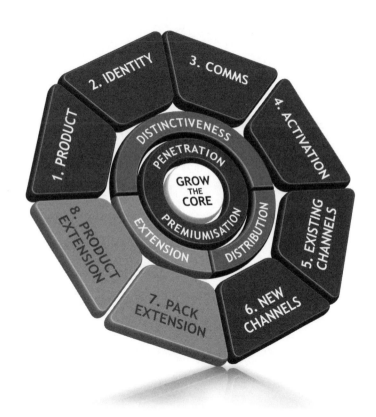

Headlines

Core range extension grows the core by adding new versions of the core product or service. By offering benefits that support a premium price, core extension can deliver a 'double whammy' of increased penetration and superior profitability. A market map can be used to highlight opportunities to deliver new benefits or meet the needs of new occasions and user groups. Core range extension can then be executed through either new pack formats or new products.

Delivering a double whammy

Core range extension offers new versions of the core product or service, such as Dove bar introducing a Refreshing Green version. You are telling new chapters of the same core brand story. This is very different from brand stretch, where you move beyond the core into totally new markets, such as Dove launching deodorants.

Core extensions help grow the core by better covering the 'market map' of benefits, occasions and target audiences (Figure 11.1). A good place to start is to ensure you have such a market map, based on qualitative and quantitative research. You can then highlight areas where your brand 'under-indexes' with less than its fair share of certain user groups or occasions. For example, the Kit-Kat chocolate brand did this work and found that it was under-represented amongst young men looking for a substantial snack. This led to the Kit-Kat Chunky core extension.

Range extension can be a great way of growing the core. It can drive penetration by widening the brand's appeal so it's relevant to more people on more occasions. But it can also deliver an additional business benefit for the core in the form of 'premiumisation': charging a higher price for new

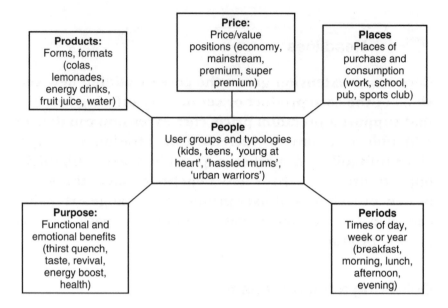

Figure 11.1: Market mapping example for soft drinks.

benefits. This means the core brand is generating more revenue for every unit sold and so driving not only volume share but also value share. As long as the new product features are genuinely adding value to the consumer, the premium price should at least recoup the extra cost of the product to maintain percentage profitability. In the best cases, the core range extension actually delivers a better percentage profit margin, meaning significantly more profit per unit sold.

A great example of this 'double whammy' of penetration and premiumisation is Gillette. The brand has been unrelenting in its drive to develop better and better razor systems. So, we have gone from Sensor (two blades) to Mach 3 (three blades) and now Fusion (five blades). As you can see from Figure 11.2, each of these is priced at a premium, supported by superior benefits. The growth in the UK core shaving business over this time is impressive:

• Razor and blade business up from £128 million in 2002 to £180 million in 2006;

Sensor	Mach 3	Fusion

| £1.00/razor | £1.70/razor | £2.19/razor |
| £4.99/5 pack | £8.49/5 pack | £8.79/4 pack |

Figure 11.2: Core extensions to drive premiumisation.

- Value share over the same period grew from 60.1% to 67.9%;
- Annual growth rate of 14%.

Watch out for cannibals

A key watch-out here is to ensure that the new version is genuinely delivering something relevant and different and so adding as much incremental business as possible. If not, the risk is 'cannibalisation' of the existing products, as happened with Crest toothpaste in the USA. The brand spent decades launching new versions such as tartar control, gum protection and whitening. However, share halved from 50% with one product to 25% with 50 products (1). Each introduction competed for the same usage occasion and introduced novelty value but not enough added value to create incremental growth. What most people wanted was an 'all-in-one' version, successfully launched by Colgate as 'Colgate Total'.

Note, there is always likely to be some cannibalisation of existing products when extending the core. This is why premiumisation is important. This way, even if the new product does steal some volume from existing products, the overall profit of the brand still goes up.

Extension or upgrade?

A second watch-out is to check there is a 'trade-off' involved to justify adding a new product, in that modifying an existing product would add a new benefit but risk undermining an existing core benefit. For example, when Head & Shoulders wanted to respond to the trend for more regular hair washing, a frequent-use version was developed with a lower amount of active ingredient and a milder cleaning system. If this had been used to replace the original version, existing users may have been disappointed with the lower efficacy and left the brand. The new product was launched as a range extension and succeeded in building sales by about 10% and attracting new users into the brand who were ready to 'trade off' efficacy for mildness.

In contrast, when the product change can improve core performance with no trade-off, upgrading the core product is a better route. For example, mainstream car makers like Ford responded to the increased demand for safety features such as ABS brakes and air bags by integrating these features into existing models. These were first offered as optional extras, creating incremental revenues, but eventually became expected in a car and so were offered as standard.

I will now introduce the two main ways of extending the core: first pack formats and then products.

Workout 7: Pack extension – WD-40

Extending through packaging formats can be a great way of growing the core. The big advantage of this form of extension is that you sell more of the same core product, rather than adding new products. You reinforce what made you famous from a brand standpoint and you increase economies of scale from a business standpoint. There are several ways pack extension can help grow your core, including solving a consumer problem and targeting new occasions and channels.

Solve a problem

One of my favourite examples of pack extension is on WD-40, the multi-purpose lubricant which stops squeaks and unlocks stuck bolts, amongst its many uses. This brilliant brand has delivered sustained and profitable growth over many years with one single core product. WD-40 used to come with a little straw taped on the side, used to help direct the spray. The problem was that people would often lose the straw. This led to the creation of 'Smart Straw', a new WD-40 pack with an integrated straw that flips up to use and back down to store (Figure 11.3). This is definitely smart on several fronts. First, this is not about making the pack look nicer or adding a gimmicky new feature. Smart Straw solves a real problem and makes the product easier to use. Second, by making WD-40 easier to use, Smart Straw creates a nice bit of news on the brand to help make the brand distinctive. This, in turn, can help drive penetration. Finally, WD-40 Smart Straw delivers the double whammy of penetration and premiumisation. It offers consumers real added value and so it's worth paying a bit more for, being sold at a premium vs. the normal can. This premium more than recoups the extra cost, making WD-40 Smart Straw more profitable. So, even if people buy it instead of a normal pack, WD-40 still makes more money. The core

Figure 11.3: Smart core extension using pack format. Reproduced by permission of WD-40 Company.

extension has become very popular with consumers, making up 15–20% of the brand's sales where it has been launched.

New occasions and channels

Range extension using packaging also has the potential to grow the core by targeting new user groups or occasions. This is a great way of breathing life into an established brand and introducing it to a whole new user base. Take Ferrero Rocher. For years, the gold-wrapped balls of chocolate wafer-encased hazelnuts have been part of the Christmas routine, or perhaps taken to dinner parties as a gift. The product was only available with a large number of units, typically 30 or 48. The brand's (in)famous 'Ambassador's party' advertising reinforced the idea of the brand being for sharing at special occasions. However, the brand has broken free of the straitjacket of special occasion usage with a new four-pack suitable for individual consumption (Figure 11.4). This is sold in newsagents' shops and at the checkouts of supermarkets. The brand is now also an indulgent, everyday treat, widening the usage of the brand and updating it. Furthermore, the four-pack has 'premiumised' the brand, with the convenience of the format supporting a premium per chocolate compared to a normal gift pack.

Figure 11.4: New formats for new occasions and channels.

Workout 8: Product extension – Ryvita

After having used new packaging formats to sell more of the existing product offer, the last step of all is to consider adding new products. Here, there is a need to focus on those products that genuinely offer potential to drive penetration by widening the brand's user base.

New occasions

McDonald's has grown its core restaurant business by increasing its appeal for the breakfast occasion, with an incredibly successful extension into fresh-ground coffee. This is priced at a premium to the bog standard coffee that was being sold. McDonald's coffee offers good quality, even beating Starbucks in some blind tests and is Rainforest Alliance certified. It's also outstanding value, with a small cappuccino from the fast-food chain costing £1.39, compared with £1.99 at Pret a Manger or £2.10 at Starbucks. Amazingly, since the 2007 launch in the UK, it has overtaken Costa Coffee to become Britain's largest seller of coffee drunk out of the home (2). This core extension has created a whole new revenue stream, with 84 million cups of coffee sold a year. Importantly, this launch has grown the core business by attracting new users into the store who might not have considered visiting a McDonald's before.

New users

Product extension can be an effective way of recruiting new users into the brand by tailoring the brand benefits to better meet their needs. An obvious example of this is the explosive growth in 'Light' products in response to increasing concerns about health. Coke Light/Diet Coke is now a bigger piece of business than Classic Coke in some markets. In beer, Bud Light has driven growth of the total Budweiser beer business, even if it has stolen some sales from the classic Bud product.

This approach can also work well in services, such as 'MORE TH>N' in the UK creating a specific insurance offer for drivers aged 18–25 called Drivetime. This offers 40% cheaper insurance for these drivers if they stay off the road between 11 p.m. and 6 a.m. – when most accidents involving young people happen. The driving is tracked by a GPS system fitted free of charge to the car.

Smart innovation on the core range is a great way of expanding the appeal of long-established, even mundane, products.

New benefits

Core range extension can help grow the core by delivering new benefits and this is especially powerful when these new benefits help premiumise the brand. A good example of this is the Ryvita brand offering three new 'seeded' versions of its crispbreads, with added sesame or sunflower seeds (Figure 11.5). These core range extensions have played a role in re-positioning the brand from being a diet product you eat out of necessity to a tasty, crunchy and healthy product you eat because you want to. The core extensions deliver a more interesting and tasty eating experience, whilst also offering extra health benefits. These extra benefits are worth paying more for, supporting a 60% price premium versus standard Ryvita.

Figure 11.5: Core extensions to premiumise.

New news

This last way of using core range extension is to add 'new news' to the brand to keep it fresh and interesting and make it more distinctive. Often, these extensions take the form of limited edition versions, which create 'urgency to buy' during the time they are on sale. This can work well in markets that have a fashion element to them, where people want the 'latest cool thing'. For example, the Axe/Lynx body spray for teenage boys launches a new fragrance concept every year. The brand team describe this as the brand launching a new 'album' each year to appeal to the new generation of users they need to attract.

This can also work well in markets that are variety driven, where people want to try new tastes, such as food. The Covent Garden brand of chilled soup is one of the best examples of this. It has gone beyond just launching the odd limited edition and has created a whole business model around a concept called 'Soup of the Month' (Figure 11.6). Each month a new soup is launched, allowing the brand to tap into seasonal produce and eating occasions. So, there

Figure 11.6: Core extensions to add new news.

is a special edition pumpkin soup for Halloween, and an English Asparagus soup when asparagus is in season. The 'Soup of the Month' brand property is now known by about 40% of the UK population, no mean feat considering it has had limited advertising support.

 Key takeouts

1. Core range extensions are a way of growing the core by adding new versions of the core product or service.
2. A market map highlights opportunities to deliver new benefits or meet the needs of new occasions and user groups.
3. The two main ways to extend the core are by offering new formats and new products.

 Checklist 11. Extend the core workplan

	Yes	No
• Have you created a market map to help identify potential opportunities for core extension?	☐	☐
• Have you first looked at pack formats as a way of extending the core, without adding extra product complexity?	☐	☐
• For the core extension ideas on the table, are they delivering enough added value to justify a premium price that at least maintains gross profit margins?	☐	☐

 Handover

You have now seen the eight core growth drivers, covering distinctiveness, distribution and core extension. The last part of the book is designed to show you how a Grow the Core project works, so you can get started on your own brand.

THE GROW THE CORE WORKPLAN

PART IV

Grow the core – getting started

 Headlines

A Grow the Core project has four key stages. This starts with an insight phase to create fuel to ignite idea creation. The lead ideas can then be brought to life and explored before being 'pitched' to the team. The final selection of ideas is based on brand and business-building potential, with these ideas being used to create the brand's marketing chapter plan.

This final chapter is designed to show you what a Growing the Core project looks like, based on the projects done by my consultancy, *the brandgym*. A typical Grow the Core project is based on four key stages: Insight, Ideas, Exploration and Action. You will see each of these in turn. An overview of the workouts is given in Figure 12.1, along with a rough idea of how long each stage should take.

Before launching into the work, there are a few things to get right from the start to increase the chances of success:

- **Who:** a cross-functional team of c.10–12 people is ideal to have a spread of talent without being so big it becomes unwieldy. This will typically cover marketing, sales, product development, consumer insight, finance and sometimes one or two people from the creative agencies on your

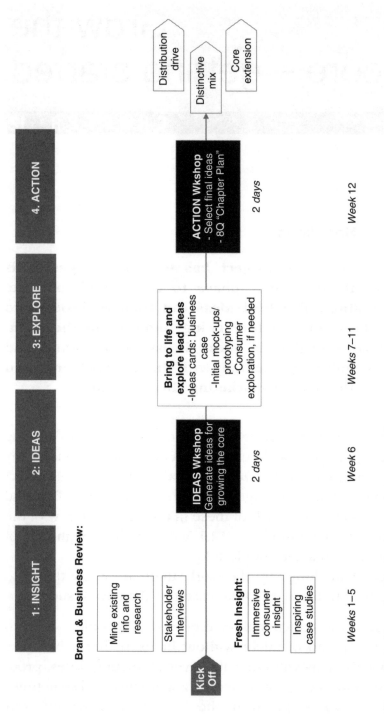

Figure 12.1: Grow the Core project workplan example.

brand. Book these people in for the key dates right at the start. It's important to have the same people throughout so they join you on a 'journey', during which they should become more aligned and engaged.

- **When:** a project should typically take no more than 12–15 weeks, with the exact time depending mainly on how much research is done. Set the dates up for the key workshops at the start and stick to them. These then work as 'drop deadlines' to push the project forward and create the sense of urgency needed to get things done.

- **Where:** the key workshops should take place in an inspiring venue away from your office to encourage fresh thinking. Book a nice big room with natural light (no basement bunkers, a sure-fire way to kill creativity). If possible, find a venue that links to the theme of your project. For example, for Carling Black Label in South Africa on a Grow the Core project linked to soccer, the workshop was done in Johannesburg's soccer stadium, with a view of the pitch.

Stage 1: Insight

This stage of the project is designed to produce insight 'fuel' that can help your team generate ideas for growing the core. A key reason for many 'brainstorming' sessions to fail is the lack of any insight, as this is like trying to launch a rocket without having any fuel on board. There are many types of insight technique that you can use, but a good place to start is to consider four different angles of attack (Figure 12.2).

Look back

Remember what made you famous

The first part of looking back is to remember what made you famous. This is a bit like 'brand archaeology'. You dig into your past marketing mix and look for hidden treasure. When was the brand 'hot', growing share and sales and when was

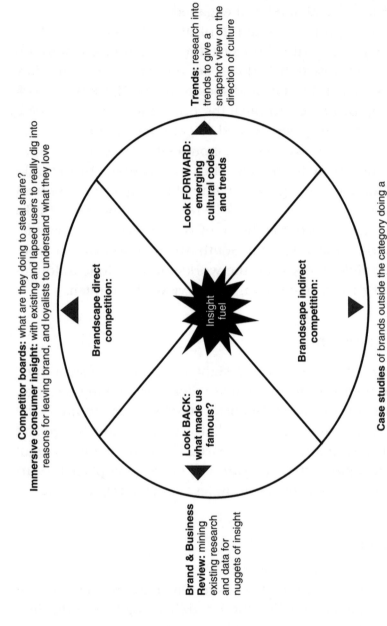

Competitor boards: what are they doing to steal share?
Immersive consumer insight: with existing and lapsed users to really dig into reasons for leaving brand, and loyalists to understand what they love

Trends: research into trends to give a snapshot view on the direction of culture

Look FORWARD: emerging cultural codes and trends

Brandscape direct competition:

Insight fuel

Brandscape indirect competition:

Look BACK: what made us famous?

Brand & Business Review: mining existing research and data for nuggets of insight

Case studies of brands outside the category doing a good job of connecting with the brand's target audience

Figure 12.2: Insight fuel for growing the core.

it 'cold'? What was the brand doing at these times? Here, you are looking for two things. Firstly, you are looking at 'the message': the content of the brand promise the brand was making. Secondly, you are looking at brand properties such as endlines, creative ideas and visual devices that were responsible for creating memory structure. Earlier in the book we saw how Hovis used this approach with its core brand communication, highlighting the 'boy on a bike' advert that it used as inspiration for a new campaign.

Brand and business review

The second part of looking back is to carry out a thorough review of the brand and business, mining all the existing data you have. On *brandgym* projects this often uncovers valuable nuggets of insight by reminding the team of key facts that have been forgotten, or by presenting data in a new and more inspiring way. There is a long list of things to look at in this stage, including brand equity tracking, split of sales by key product (to help follow the money) and qualitative research. An example of the data sources for a real-life *brandgym* project is shown in Table 12.1.

One key chart that has often proven to be an eye-opener is the analysis of business by product line, in terms of revenue, gross profit and sales growth (Figure 12.3). This is often a powerful reminder of the importance of the core, and often shows up smaller products that have been stealing budget and talent from the core.

Consumer feedback

Consumer panels can be a good source of ideas for growing the core. With the rise of digital media, many brands now have online panels they can use, with the most advanced perhaps being mystarbucks.com. Consumer feedback forms can also be a fantastic form of free insight, provided you take the time to read and act on them. One company that did this is Pret a Manger, the leading UK sandwich shop chain.

Table 12.1: Brand and business review example

Data Source	Use of Data in Insight Mining
1. Business data	
— Revenue, gross profit and net profit for past 3 years	— Understand overall health of the business
— Market share data vs. competition vs. ago for past 3 years	— Understand overall health of the business
— Growth and split of revenue and gross profit by product	— 'Follow the money': highlight core of the business and potential 'dwarf' products
2. Research	
— User profile (age, sex etc.) vs. population and competition	— Help identify core target consumer
— Quantitative brand tracking: awareness, image, usage	— Brand health and identifying areas of brand image strength and weakness
— Shopper date: penetration, frequency of purchase etc.	— Highlight current core strength and opportunities for growth
— Usage and attitude study	— Identify key consumer drivers on the core
— In-depth qualitative work on brand	— Understand in-depth current consumer imagery of the brand
— Trends work done	— Identify key trends affecting the core: opportunities and issues
3. Brand mix	
— Visual of product range and pack history over time	— Understand key visual equities
— Blind product testing + full set of products to try	— Understand product performance: strengths = brand truths to build on + issues to address
— Photos of point-of-sale + store checks	— See brand presence at point of purchase
— Listings/facings/distribution by retailer	— Review current physical availability
— Pricing for key products vs. competition	— Understand value position
— Media spend/promo spend evolution	— Understand share of voice, how well brand is being kept top of mind
4. Brand vision and positioning	
— Current brand vision/positioning: brand book, video etc.	— Understand current brand story, use as inspiration to grow the core ideas
5. Marketing plans	
— Marketing plan on a page for last 3 years	— Understand key chapters of activity and how budget is being spent
— Activity review: worked well, less well, key brand properties	— Identify key brand properties and mix elements
— Historical reel of comms work as far back as possible (min 10 yrs)	— Identify what made the brand famous, brand story and brand properties

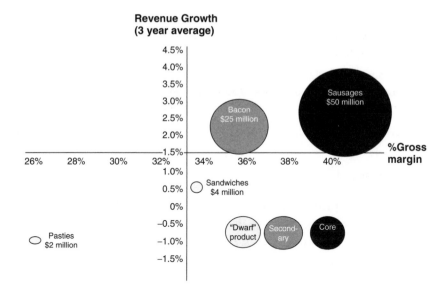

Figure 12.3: 'Following the money' for a food company.
(Source: author's own)

Figure 12.4: Consumer feedback to grow the core.

A cup of fresh soup had this note from the CEO on the side (Figure 12.4):

A while ago, a consumer phoned me to say our soup was good but not amazing. The gauntlet was down. I tracked down and engaged (full-time) the UK's premier soup guru and cookbook writer, Nick Sandler. Together we changed our recipes, our stock, our ingredients and cooking methods. We took on and trained new soup chefs.

Thank you to that lady who called (sorry but I've lost your number). If you're reading this, I hope you agree we rose to the challenge. Do let me know what you think, and thanks again.

Signed, Julian Metcalfe

Look forward

At the same time as rewinding to look at what made your brand famous in the past and what built its strong brand associations, there is also a need to look to the future and how the world is changing. For example, on Carling Black Label this involved looking at how expressions of masculinity were evolving in South Africa. This work was done by analysing communication in the form of advertising, but also popular culture such as TV programmes and movies. This work was a key input into creating an expression of masculine achievement that was more aspirational. This was based on success in different forms of life, both professional and personal, in contrast with the previous brand expression that was based on physical achievement.

Direct competition

There is, of course, a need to look at the brand's direct competition, to highlight potential opportunities and threats. Also, this analysis helps the team work on ensuring that the core brand mix is distinctive versus the key competitors. This means the competitive analysis needs to look not only at brand positioning but also the key brand properties of other brands in the marketplace.

Another insight tool that has worked well has been 'immersive insight' with the target consumer to understand the brand and how it's doing vs. competition, with both existing and lapsed or non-users. This involves talking to and observing consumers at home or out and about using the product or service, rather than watching them in the artificial confines of a focus group facility. This technique can create very rich insight, as people are not trying to remember what they do and how they use products, as they have to in a focus group. A leading coffee company looking at coffee consumption outside the home in cafés and coffee shops learnt a huge amount from using this technique. One key insight concerned the importance of the whole coffee drinking experience and showed the team that the coffee beans they sold were but one small part of this. The cup the coffee was served in, the ambience and the amount of froth on the cappuccino were all vital. This made the team realise it had to do more to help its customers create an 'end-to-end' experience to build the brand, and not just focus on selling the quality of the coffee.

Indirect competition

One of the most inspiring forms of insight on Growing the Core projects has been doing case studies on 'peer group' brands. These are brands from outside your category that are doing a good job of delivering similar benefits to the ones you want and/or connecting well with the core target audience. For example, when working on the Ryvita crispbread brand, the key challenge was to appeal to women 30–50 years old, and to reposition the brand from being a 'punitive' diet food to an enjoyable and healthy food. Part of this re-launch was to create a more aspirational brand personality. Looking at the Diet Coke and Special K brands helped a lot, leading to the idea of Ryvita needing to be like 'one of the girls': less solo and more sociable, a food you're not shy of eating in front of other women. This helped inspire new communication showing three girlfriends discussing toppings for Ryvita at the same time as sharing gossip. This played a key role in helping revitalise the brand and getting it growing again.

Stage 2: Ideas

This critical stage of the project is where the team will work on generating a long list of ideas for growing the core. Typically, this stage is centred on an Ideas Workshop with the projects team meeting taking place over two days. A rough idea of how this sort of workshop unfolds is as follows:

Day One (9 a.m. – 6 p.m.)

- Recap objectives and workplan;
- Share Grow the Core principles and the key core growth drivers (Activation, Communication, Identity, Product, Upgrading the Core, Distribution, Core extension);
- Share brand and business review => use to generate core growth ideas;
- Share fresh insight 1 (e.g. immersive consumer work) => use to generate core growth ideas;
- Share fresh insight 2 (e.g. brand peer group case studies) => use to generate core growth ideas;
- Review all the ideas generated and do initial prioritisation based on potential to grow the core => get to the c. Top 10 ideas).

Day Two (9 a.m. – 1 p.m.)

- Review of the Top 10 ideas (one page per idea), which have been worked up overnight (polished, sharpened);
- Split into pairs and work up a more detailed summary of the idea;
- Agree the brief for bringing to life and exploring the ideas;
- Next steps.

Stage 3: Exploration

This stage of the project is where you bring to life and explore your ideas for growing the core. This can take the form of simply exploring the lead ideas inside the business and getting feedback or it can involve doing qualitative or even quantitative consumer research. Whichever route you take, there are two key ways of bringing to life the ideas.

Prototypes

The old adage that 'a picture is worth a thousand words' is definitely true when it comes to ideas for growing the core and for marketing in general. On *brandgym* projects we work with partner design agencies to mock up ideas for growing the core, to help explore them with consumers and present them internally in a way which is inspiring. On a recent project for a chilled food brand we did mock-ups of new pack designs, new premium core extensions, a revamped website home page and distinctive activation ideas, and the product team also worked up prototype products to taste.

Idea cards

The second bit of work for each idea is to create a simple one-page summary of the idea to capture what it is, why consumers would buy it and what I call a 'beer mat business plan': a rough idea of the growth potential for the core, in terms of incremental revenue and gross profit. This approach forces the team to make short and snappy presentations, rather than the typical 20–30 pages of PowerPoint. It also makes it much easier to compare the different ideas, by using a consistent format. A typical idea card format is shown in Table 12.2.

Stage 4: Action

The key findings from the exploration stage on the lead ideas are taken into the Action Workshop, another two-day off-site session with the core team. In this workshop, we take an approach like the TV programme *The Dragons' Den*

Table 12.2: Grow the Core idea card

GROW THE CORE IDEA CARD

WHAT: what is the Grow the Core idea: e.g. Product? Packaging? Activation?
....
....

WHY: why will people want to buy it?
....
....

WHERE: where will people buy it?
....

WHEN: EARLIEST possible launch date..
RECOMMENDED launch date ....

BRINGING TO LIFE THE BRAND:	LO	OK	HI
- Brand benefit	☐	☐	☐
- Brand reason to believe	☐	☐	☐
- Brand personality	☐	☐	☐
- Brand values...............................	☐	☐	☐
- Using key brand properties..........	☐	☐	☐
OVERALL BRAND-NESS	Lo	OK	Hi

BEERMAT BUSINESS PLAN

- Consumer appeal:	Lo	OK	Hi
- Differentiation:	Lo	OK	Hi
	Lo	OK	Hi

- Sales Mill Euros (3yrs): ☐
- Gross profit margin %: ☐

- OVERALL BUSINESS POTENTIAL:	Lo	OK	Hi

(*Shark Tank* in the USA). This involves getting the team to think and act like a group of venture capitalists, who have a limited amount of capital to invest. A rough idea of how this sort of workshop unfolds is as follows:

Day One (9 a.m. – 6 p.m.)

- Recap objectives and workplan;
- Team members 'pitch' the lead ideas for growing the core, using the idea cards and prototypes;
- Capture feedback on each idea;
- Plot the ideas on a brand and business-building matrix;
- 'Place your bets' exercise to select top three to four ideas.

Day Two (9 a.m. – 1 p.m.)

- Review of the top three to four ideas which have been worked up overnight (polished, sharpened);
- Working up a draft eight-quarter marketing chapter plan, which sequences the lead Grow the Core ideas;
- Next steps.

Place your bets

Grow the Core ideas are then 'pitched' by team members who try to secure backing for their ideas, using the idea cards and prototypes, with no more than five to ten minutes per idea. A huge wallchart is used to map the ideas, typically based on the brand and business-building potential (Figure 12.5). You can pick different dimensions if you prefer. This helps identify how strong each idea is:

1. **'Cash builders':** deliver profit for the core, but don't do much for the brand image, such as Gillette launching plastic razors to compete with Bic. A brand can do a few of these projects, but they are ideally executed with very limited marketing, so you can focus resources on 'hero' ideas.
2. **'Heros':** these ideas *dramatise* the brand positioning while generating profitable and significant business growth for the core. Examples would be core range extensions like Gillette's Fusion, or upgrading the core

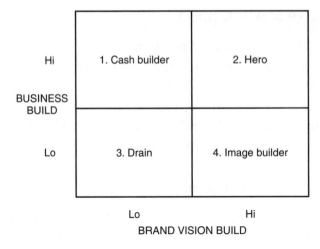

Figure 12.5: Place your bets – brand and business-building matrix.

ideas such as Galaxy chocolate, dramatising smoothness via a new smoother shape of chocolate tablet, improved packaging and new communication.

3. **'Drains':** would eat up resources and have a limited impact on either brand image or business growth.

4. **'Image builders':** ideas that look small in terms of incremental growth on the core, yet do something positive for the brand. Covent Garden's Soup of the Month could fall into this category. However, these are the most risky type of ideas in some ways, as they often eat up resources without delivering the expected image-building effects.

To arrive at the final shortlist of around three to four ideas, the team members are asked to 'place their bets' by allocating an imaginary budget (e.g. £3 million) of venture capital to no more than three ideas.

Chapter plan

Having placed your bets to identify the lead ideas for growing the core, the next and final step is to have a first go at the

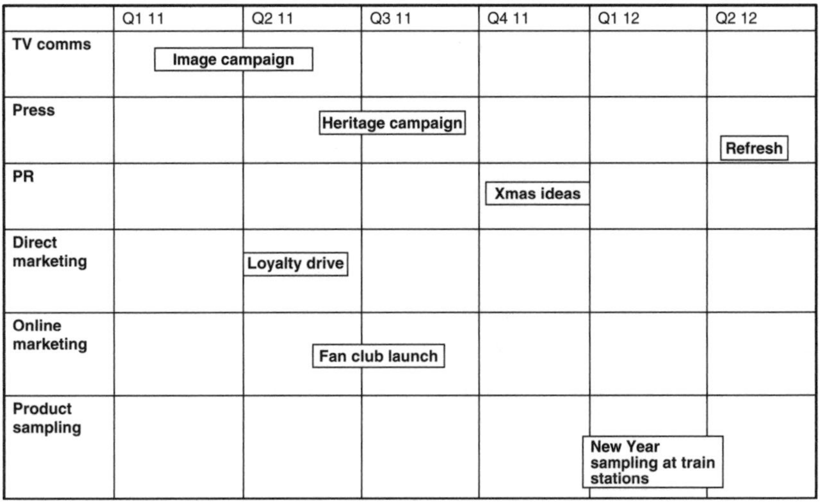

	Q1 11	Q2 11	Q3 11	Q4 11	Q1 12	Q2 12
TV comms		Image campaign				
Press			Heritage campaign			Refresh
PR				Xmas ideas		
Direct marketing		Loyalty drive				
Online marketing			Fan club launch			
Product sampling					New Year sampling at train stations	

Figure 12.6: Conventional marketing plan.

marketing chapter plan. This is different to a conventional plan that is developed in a 'horizontal' fashion. Down the left-hand side you have different bits of the mix; along the top you have months of the year; horizontal strips are used to show marketing activity and how much money is being spent on each (Figure 12.6). The risk here is that each bit of the mix, and each agency creating it, is working in a separate 'silo'. This can lead to fragmentation and dilution of the brand message. An effort to get the same look, feel and slogan may be used but tends to be a superficial attempt at integration.

Brand chapters can help you build a marketing plan in a different way, to deliver more bang for your buck and make the process more inspiring for the business. We start with each idea that brings to life the brand idea and grows the core, and treat this as one chapter of the brand story. We then work *down* the marketing plan on the role of different elements of the mix (Figure 12.7). Here, different parts of the mix (TV, press, PR, Facebook, blogging) are not just joined

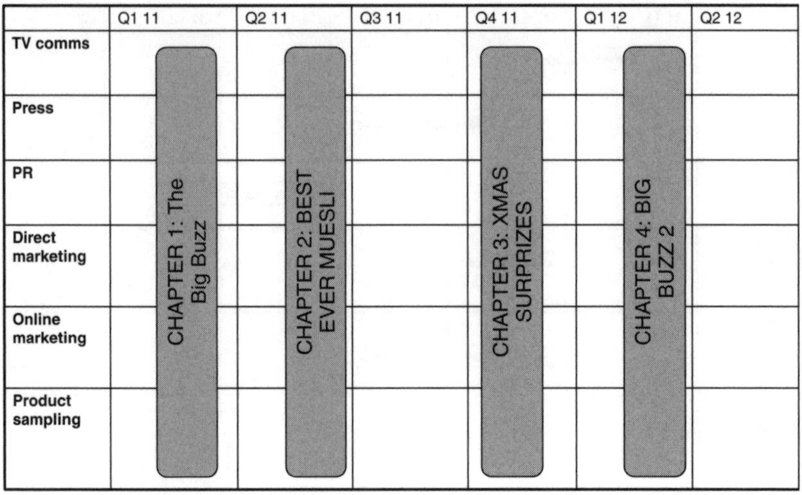

	Q1 11	Q2 11	Q3 11	Q4 11	Q1 12	Q2 12
TV comms						
Press						
PR	CHAPTER 1: The Big Buzz	CHAPTER 2: BEST EVER MUESLI		CHAPTER 3: XMAS SURPRIZES	CHAPTER 4: BIG BUZZ 2	
Direct marketing						
Online marketing						
Product sampling						

Figure 12.7: Brand chapter plan.

up so they look and feel the same, they are orchestrated to increase the effectiveness of one another. We go beyond integration to 'amplification' of the mix.

 Key takeouts

1. Insight fuel is key to ignite idea creation for growing the core, combining a thorough review of the brand and business and fresh insight into the brand and consumer.
2. Bring to life ideas using mock-ups and prototypes, to help explore them both internally and with consumers.
3. The lead ideas can then be pitched as if presenting to a venture capital fund, to select the lead ideas with which to create a marketing chapter plan for the core.

Checklist 12. Grow the Core workplan

	Yes	No
• Have you created a multi-functional team of c. 10–12 people and booked them for the key workshops?	☐	☐
• Have you created insight fuel to inspire idea creation, using both a brand and business review and fresh insight (look back and look forward)?	☐	☐
• Do you have a plan to bring to life the lead ideas using mock-ups and prototypes?	☐	☐

 ## Handover

You have now reached the end of Grow the Core. *Hopefully, by now you have a good feel for both the principles and practicalities of growing the core. The last chapter has given you an idea of how to get started with work to grow your core business. Go to the* brandgym *blog (www.brandgymblog.com) to get loads more examples, including visual case studies. And do please get in touch if you have ideas to add or questions to ask at david@thebrandgym.com*

References

Introduction

1   Zook, C. and Allen, J. (2001) *Profit From the Core*, Harvard Business Press

Chapter 1

1   http://responsibility.timberland.com

Chapter 2

1   www.apple.com
2   Haig, M. (2003) *Brand Failures: the truth about the 100 biggest branding mistakes of all time*, Kogan Page
3   http://www.thesundaytimes.co.uk
4   Zook, C. and Allen, J. (2001) *Profit From the Core*, Harvard Business Press

Chapter 3

1   Marketing Success Through Differentiation – of Anything, *Harvard Business Review*, January/February 1980 (Reprint)
2   Zook, C. and Allen, J. (2001) *Profit From the Core*, Harvard Business Press

Chapter 4

1   Sharp, B. (2010) *How Brands Grow*, Oxford University Press
2   http://mweigel.typepad.com/canalside-view
3   http://byronsharp.wordpress.com
4   http://www.warc.com
5   http://en.wikipedia.org

Chapter 5

1   Smith, G. (1992) *Lucozade: A Case History*, IPA Advertising Effectiveness Paper
2   http://www.fortune.com
3   http://www.ft.com
4   http://ar2010.tomtom.com

Chapter 6

1   Boguski, A. and Winsor, J. (2009) *Baked In*, Agate Publishing
2   http://www.thetimes.co.uk
3   http://www.brandrepublic.com

Chapter 7

1   http://www.nytimes.com
2   Golding, D. (Editor) (2010) *Advertising Works 19*, WARC

Chapter 8

1   http://brandautopsy.typepad.com
2   'How Dove changed the rules of the beauty game', *Market Leader*, Winter 2005, 43–46
3   'How real curves can grow your brand', *Viewpoint*, Number 9, April 2005, 16–20
4   http://www.thinkbox.tv
5   http://www.decodemarketing.co.uk
6   Rimini, M. (Editor) (2003) *Advertising Works 12*, WARC
7   http://www.brandrepublic.com
8   http://www.advfn.com
9   *As good today as it has ever been*, IPA 2009 Effectiveness Awards Paper, MBCD
10 http://byronsharp.wordpress.com
11 http://blogs.wsj.com/speakeasy
12 http://www.slideshare.net
13 http://adage.com/article/digital
14 http://www.brandrepublic.com
15 http://www.independent.co.uk/news
16 http://mashable.com

Chapter 9

1   http://inside.nike.com/blogs

Chapter 10

1   http://en.wikipedia.org
2   http://www.brandrepublic.com
3   http://www.thetimes.co.uk
4   http://www.ifoapplestore.com
5   http://www.istockanalyst.com
6   http://www.telegraph.co.uk/finance

Chapter 11

1   Haig, M. (2003) *Brand Failures: the truth about the 100 biggest branding mistakes of all time*, Kogan Page
2   http://www.telegraph.co.uk/finance

Also by

By David Taylor and David Nichols

The brandgym: A practical workout to boost brand business (new edition)

By David Taylor

Brand Stretch: Why 1 in 2 extensions fail and how to beat the odds
Brand Vision: Energize your team to drive brand and business growth
Never Mind the Sausage, Where's the Sizzle?

By David Nichols

Return on Ideas: A practical guide to making innovation pay

Index